WEARABLE

ART

FOR

REAL

PEOPLE

WEARABLE

ART

FOR

REAL

PEOPLE

MARY MASHUTA

C&T PUBLISHING

© Copyright 1989 by Mary Mashuta

Photography by Sharon Risedorph
San Francisco, California

Editing by Sayre Van Young
Berkeley, California

Design/Production Coordination by Bobbi Sloan Design
Berkeley, California

Illustrations by Marilyn Hill
San Pablo, California

Typesetting by Byron Brown/MACAW
Oakland, California

Published by C&T Publishing
5021 Blum Road, #1
Martinez, CA 94553

ISBN: 0-914881-24-8

Library of Congress Catalog Card Number: 89-60484

Printed in Hong Kong

My dedication is threefold: to my family, who has been supportive through the whole process; to my students, who have asked, "what would happen if...?"; and to Mendo and Kasten, who have kept me company through the long hours.

CONTENTS

The Color Section follows page 40.

INTRODUCTION

The quilt world has come a long way since the first Fairfield Processing/Concord Fabrics Fashion Show in Houston in 1979. I too have grown personally and artistically since the relatively simple vests I created for the second and third shows. For the 1987/88 show, I created a piece that went with one of my story quilts, "Make-believe Summer: At the Beach." It is fun, it is outrageous, and there is no way I will ever fit into the shorts and halter top that were part of the outfit! But then the Fairfield show is a chance to pull out all the stops and just *be* outrageous, a time to forget about personal figure limitations and design for a perfect size 10.

For the second Paducah Fashion Show, I submitted an understated ensemble, "Akasaka," made from Japanese stripes. To my surprise, it placed fourth, pretty good for an outfit which, if not understated by "street" standards, certainly was by "runway" standards. Even in these big shows, there is an opportunity for garments that simply say, "less is more."

When I began thinking about *Wearable Art for Real People*, I asked myself some tough questions before I started the actual process of writing. Basically I considered why I like doing decorative clothing, what keeps other quilters from trying wearables, and what is special about creating this type of clothing. In my answers, I found reinforcement for my reasons for writing about and sharing some of the things I've learned through my years of creating and teaching. I hope you will enjoy reading this book (the result of those years of creating and teaching), looking at the photos and illustrations, and figuring how you can apply the ideas here to your own creations, whether for the runway or for more casual settings.

Here are the questions—and my answers—that helped me understand more fully my feelings about wearable art. You might consider your own answers to each question before reading mine.

Why have I always been interested in wearable art when I consider myself a quilter?
- Wearable art provides an opportunity to try out quilting patterns, designs, and techniques in a smaller format.
- It gives me a fighting chance of finishing a project.
- I enjoy wearing my creations and receiving compliments (we're being honest here!).
- It supplies a way to express my own uniqueness.
- I know there is something special in my closet to wear to quilting events.
- Wearable art allows me to combine my knowledge of sewing and custom dressmaking with an art form I love.

What keeps many people from the enjoyment of creating wearables?
- They are self-conscious about perceived body imperfections.
- They're unsure whether to select commercial patterns or those designed specifically for quilters.
- They wonder whether the garment will fit when finished.
- They are planning to go on a diet soon, and quilted garments just make one look larger, anyway.
- They're afraid the garment will wear them, rather than them wearing the garment.
- They're uncertain what colors look best on them.
- They wonder where the garment could be worn appropriately.
- They lack confidence in their sewing skills.

What unique challenges do wearables offer?
- Wearables are a stimulus for imagination and creativity.
- Wearables offer an opportunity for a new design format, a chance to create in three dimensions rather than two.
- Wearables offer new exercises in employing the design principles.
- Wearables let one try quilting techniques (machine quilting, biscuits, tucking) that may be more appropriate or suitable for clothing than for a quilt.
- Wearables provide a reason to use fabrics not generally used in quilts.
- Wearables let one experiment with different battings, quilting possibilities, and finishing techniques.
- Wearables are a different way to express what is special about oneself.

HOW TO USE THIS BOOK

This book follows the conception and development of garments using three different fabric/color concepts: pushed neutrals, hand-dyed fabrics, and stripes. For each, we'll look closely at the kinds of fabric and color involved, how to creatively use them in designing garments, and then consider appropriate embellishments. Some technical advice along the way will make your sewing adventures a little easier, too.

Use this book as a starting point, or to supplement or check the knowledge you already have. Nothing pleases me more than when a workshop participant takes an idea I have presented and runs with it, coming up with something new all her own. As a teacher, my reward comes from planting the seed that triggers a creative thought or expression. In fact, one of the ideas presented here came about because a student misheard my directions and invented a variation of an old technique.

I know you want to get right to the "good stuff," the pictures and the designing. But if you need some help in selecting specific supplies such as patterns or fabrics, consult Chapter 5. If you need assistance with specific sewing techniques, see Chapter 6. But first of all, finding the fabric you'll use….

I am lucky to live in the San Francisco Bay Area where fabric is readily available in quilt and other fabric shops. Since I also attend many quilt-related merchant malls, including Houston Festival, I am exposed to and can purchase a wider variety of materials than you may feel is available where you live. If, for instance, you can't buy Japanese striped fabric locally, just apply the basic information here to the stripes already in your fabric collection, then watch for additional unusual stripes to purchase. Mail-order fabrics can be a wonderful resource. For example, my sister, Roberta Horton, has designed several groups of stripes and plaids; they're primarily for quilt-making, but some of her fabrics would also work well in garments. My "Shibui Stripes," designed for the Cotton Patch, are also available through mail order. Consult the Appendix (under the Cotton Patch) for the address.

If your local quilt store doesn't carry hand-dyed fabric, you can suggest they carry it, order it yourself, or take a class in fabric dyeing. You don't necessarily have to have hand-dyed fabric to make fabric puffs or biscuits; they can be folded in a variety of different fabrics.

Perhaps your quilt store doesn't even carry a wide assortment of solid cotton fabrics. Again, a variety of fabric—even solid cottons—can be ordered from mail-order vendors. You can also teach yourself to systematically add possible colors to your fabric collection as you shop. Once you have a "perceptual set" to see certain colors, you may be pleasantly surprised to find that the fabrics were always there—you just didn't notice them.

I'm reminded of the experience of two of my students who, after a daylong outing with their children, began comparing notes. They discovered that one had seen pushed-neutral color schemes all day; the other had seen potential piecing designs. Each had selected a different "perceptual set" to use while spending the day in the same environment! You simply see what you think you are going to see.

You may be disappointed because I didn't include a single pattern in this book. Being realistic, there is no way I could come up with a pattern to please or fit everyone. I don't particularly enjoy drafting patterns even though I've had courses in both pattern drafting and French draping. I far prefer "fooling around" with commercial patterns and making minor changes and adjustments to suit my needs.

I have also not included specific pattern adjustments for all the standard figure problems, but instead have highlighted several problems that consistently crop up in workshops. The Bibliography lists an excellent book, *Power Sewing* by Sandra Betzina, if you want more information on pattern adjustments. Further, even though most garments in this book were made from commercial patterns, I have not included any pattern numbers. By the time you read this, the patterns will no doubt be discontinued, since frequent change seems to be the only constant in the pattern business.

It helps to have realistic personal goals for each project—don't try to reinvent the wheel every time (nor build Rome in a day!). I want to see some growth and development in each new project I tackle. I always try at least one new concept, idea, color scheme, fabric, or technique, but everything doesn't have to be new for me to be happy with the project. Even the most famous and accomplished quilter had to learn, and practice, and grow. No one just wakes up one morning doing wonderful things.

Pick a project of manageable size, one that you have a fighting chance of finishing. The energy from the exhilaration of completion can be used as bonus energy to start another project. Focus on attainable goals; that's how the professionals get so much done, despite busy, hectic schedules.

To the old adage, "The more you do, the more you can do," I would add its corollary: "The less you do, the less you can do." I find that the more garments and quilts I make, the faster I can design new ones. The first really unique vest I made took six months of thought and work; the last one—far more complex—was completed in two weeks and had matching pants. Make a list of personal sewing goals, and be sure words such as "completion" and "finish" appear!

One last thought: Play is an important part of creativity. Learn to ask, "What would happen if...?" Sometimes we become overly concerned with the "preciousness" of the fabric and this inhibits us from taking chances with it. You may have to sacrifice some fabric, but consider the possibilities: you risk a little time and a little cloth—your reward may well be something truly creative and unique.

1

THE WEARABLES CONCEPT AND PERSONAL ATTRIBUTES

Your personal attributes are what make you different from everyone else. They are what make you rare, peculiar, one-of-a-kind. And what are the things that make you special, that set you apart, when you want to create wearables? Consider the following four ways to evaluate yourself; they'll help you determine what kind of wearables project will work best for you:

Skill level
Body uniqueness
Flamboyance quotient
Time commitment

SKILL LEVEL

Although it's important to match your skill level with what you're expecting of yourself, it's just as important to stretch and try new things. The women who made the garments in this book possessed quite different skill levels. For some, it was their first wearable; others are willing—and able—to sell their work. Despite their different skill levels, each one was eager to stretch—a little or a lot—to make something new.

When asked to classify *your* sewing expertise, there are several possible responses. A beginner might reply:

1. I'm *not* very good, or
2. I'm *not* very good *yet,* or
3. I'm *just* learning, or
4. I'm learning *and* trying new things, or
5. I'm learning and *enjoy* trying new things.

I would much rather teach a 5 than a 1. Both might have exactly the same skill level, but they feel so differently about it. One appears to feel inferior, inadequate, and probably overwhelmed. The other knows that she still has a lot to master, but she is willing to try, and enjoys the trying.

The techniques and ideas presented here are of varying complexity. Designs can be simplified; individual design segments made larger. Every square inch of the garment doesn't have to be covered with piecing. You can feature something that was difficult for you to do skillwise in a major area where it will show and fill in the rest of the garment with something less complex. In this way, you get the maximum mileage from your efforts.

If you are a beginner, work on improving your skills as well as your design and color sense. For example, work on learning to cut and sew accurately. If templates are involved, take the time to draw the individual pieces and add the seam allowances precisely. Spot check individual pieces to make sure you are cutting them accurately. Precision and accuracy cannot be overemphasized.

Some of our personal attributes are difficult or impossible to change. At least skill level is an area we can have some control over, if we want. When you master your craft, it gives you the tools to carry out what you want to do designwise.

BODY UNIQUENESS

We quilters, especially, face one of the hardest lessons in life: learning to accept the body we received. No one seems to be happy, but short of a dye job, another diet, more exercise, liposuction, and plastic surgery, things aren't really going to change very much. Alas, it is far easier to find fault with ourselves than it is to list our positive attributes.

Yet I firmly believe anyone who wants to can wear a decorative garment. And you don't have to have a Miss America or runway model figure; few quilters do. As a group we are far too sedentary. There's simply no way to get a quilt quilted or a garment created and spend hours chasing tennis balls around the court.

So take a little time to list your "good" or at least "acceptable" physical attributes; it will focus your attention on the plus column, rather than the negatives. When making a garment, look for ways to maximize your positive qualities. For example, select colors that flatter your coloring, or pick styles that play up the good features of your build.

Next, consider what you would prefer *not* to focus attention on. For example, the majority of us think we have disproportionately big hips. (Take heart—the *average* American woman is one to two sizes larger on the bottom half!) How do you minimize hips? Be sure that skirts or pants fit well, and that they aren't too tight. That only emphasizes bulges. Make this part of the body as neutral as possible; this is not the place to make a bold fashion statement. Clothe the hips in a supportive, background color, and use color and interesting details to draw the eye elsewhere.

If you are large in the bust area, apply a similar solution. Neutralize the area by making the design and color in the area supportive. Direct the viewer's eye up to the face with color and design details such as V-necks. An all-over design calls less attention to individual body parts than one with clearly definable special spots.

Scale the individual pattern pieces to your body size. A smaller woman has to be particularly careful to not overwhelm herself. On the other hand, a larger woman can carry off the use of bigger individual pieces.

What you wear with a vest or jacket makes a big difference. If you prefer to not call attention to your body size or shape, avoid or at least limit abrupt color changes. Look at Color Plates 13 and 14 showing Dorothy Clarke in her pushed-neutral vest, "Urban Lilacs." She selected a skirt color to harmonize with the vest color, and then purchased two T-shirts to wear with the outfit. The darker lavender one has a more formal appearance because it matches the skirt color. It also provides a more neutral background: the eye doesn't have to notice differences in hue or value. When Dorothy wears the vest with the lighter colored shirt, the outfit looks more informal. The viewer is more aware of individual body parts because of the color change. If Dorothy switched to a white blouse, this effect would be exaggerated even further.

It's not necessary that everything match perfectly. Notice the vest "Desert Sky," in Color Plate 7, by Roz Zinns. Her skirt and blouse don't match exactly, but they blend in a pleasing way not only with each other, but with Roz's vest (the star of the ensemble).

An important part of color is value, that is, how light and dark is perceived. In designing wearables for the runway, strong value contrast is used because the piece is viewed from a distance. If you want to create more understated, wearable clothing, or if you are trying to achieve an all-over flowing feeling, such extreme value contrast may not be necessary or even desired. Rather than having a dramatic light-dark contrast, try a dark-medium or a medium-light contrast.

Another kind of body uniqueness is your personal coloring. In California, it's popular to have one's personal colors "done," that is, to consult a trained color expert for advice about what colors will make one look good, and what colors create a dramatic, understated, or neutral look.

For example, indigo blue is one of my neutral colors. I often wear jeans skirts made from indigo-dyed fabric because this color makes me feel calm. For me, a jeans skirt and matching top act as a neutral background when I team them with a more dramatically colored vest. Your neutral or dramatic colors may well be totally different from mine. And though consulting a color expert can be great fun, it isn't essential. Consider what colors make you feel calmer or more centered; what color do you wear most often when you want to "set off" something? On the other hand, what color were you wearing when everyone raved about your "new" blouse (even if it is ten years old)—that may be the dramatic, special color for you. And remember too, while the colors of an outfit interact with each other, they also interact with one's skin, eye, and hair colors. A veritable symphony!

You are also different from others because you may live in a different climate or be in a different life stage. Those in warmer climates will want to be careful about creating bulky, quilted garments that are often too warm to wear comfortably. Asymmetrically closing vests and jackets are exciting designwise, but they don't look as good when worn open. Garments with traditional center openings provide a way to fashionably cool off while still wearing the garment.

Similarly, if hot flashes are a part of your life, consider that you carry around your own warmer climate! When a hot flash occurs, you'll want to cool off without calling undue attention to yourself—less heavy layers and center openings on your vests or jackets will make maintaining your personal air conditioning a little easier.

FLAMBOYANCE QUOTIENT

Your flamboyance quotient is another way to decide what is special about you. Do you consider yourself an introvert or an extrovert; is your personality more dramatic or more understated? Do you want the attention to focus on you or would you prefer to be in the background?

After going to all the trouble to create a wearable garment, you want to feel comfortable while wearing it. It is important that *you* wear your clothes, rather than having them wear you. Keeping your flamboyance quotient in mind helps you to decide how outrageous to be in your creating, and when it's time to calm things down a bit.

Consider personal coloring in tandem with your flamboyance quotient when planning an ensemble or an outfit that includes your wearable. For me, garments based on indigo, one of my neutrals, are more understated. If I want to create a somewhat more flashy statement, I can combine turquoise or aqua, two of my dramatic colors.

TIME COMMITMENT

How often I've heard someone say "I can't—I just don't have enough time." Time and its management are a concern most of us share. However, you've probably also heard the old adage, "If you want something done, ask a busy person." It's not necessarily those with the most time who get the most created. Quilters with less time available who produce more, do so because they learn to manage their time better. They don't fritter it away, and they are constantly on the lookout for faster, more efficient methods.

One thing that helps me is to have a specific completion date in mind when beginning a project. For me this could be a local or national show, or an upcoming symposium where I'll want something new to wear. If this brings back memories of high school and going down to the wire on papers and assignments, remember we all usually did meet those deadlines.

Think about the varied tasks necessary to complete a project. Some require solitary quiet time, while other tasks can be completed with people around you. Make appointments with yourself for the solitary quiet time just as you would pencil-in a dental appointment on your calendar. (For further encouragement, read the Statue of Liberty contest book, *All Flags Flying*.)

Look closely at the process of making a garment and decide which parts you most enjoy. For example, if you don't like to hand quilt, learn to machine quilt or limit yourself to a minimal amount of hand quilting in your project. Do more of what you like, and less of what you don't like.

If you are short on time and really want to complete a garment, create something interesting for the major area and then figure out a method with less of a time commitment for minor areas. The twin goals are completion *and* creation—something you've enjoyed working on. Frustration and feeling overwhelmed are not part of the process.

2

PUSHED
NEUTRALS

The concept of the "pushed-neutral" color scheme was developed in the early 1980s. At that time, the fashionable decorating colors were neutrals—various grays and beiges that were, in fact, soon to evolve into the "No Color" look. (This was just prior to the "Southwest" look.) In my professional interior design work, I had become interested in the soft, subtle differences possible when neutrals were combined. On the other hand, in my quilt work, I was frustrated because I could never find matching gradated shades of grays, beiges, or similar muted colors. Like most quilters, I wanted my colors to match. This was before I realized that they would be far more interesting if they didn't.

One day I decided to purchase all the solid grays and beiges I could find in my two local quilt stores. I was going to stop worrying about what I couldn't have and see if I could figure out a way to work with what *was* available. I challenged myself to use as many of them as I could in a vest.

Knowing that a vest was imminent, I began sketching geometric motifs I noticed while on a train ride between northern and southern California. The ride took considerably longer than expected, so I was able to collect many design motifs—from upholstery, carpets, handbags and totes, and people's clothing. When it came time to start piecing, I had my design inspirations in my notebook and my stack of fabrics before me. "Amtrak-Am-Slow" was born, the first example of the use of repetitive designs in the pushed-neutral color scheme. (See Color Plates 1 through 3.)

A few years later, I devised another approach to using the same color scheme—a modular approach. Parked in front of my television tuned to Alistair Cooke's "America" series celebrating the birthday of the Statue of Liberty, I invented my "Eucalyptus" vest. (See Color Plates 4 through 6.) I ended up celebrating as an American and as a garment designer!

Now I had two basic approaches to using the pushed-neutral color scheme. In the first, one creates a series of motifs and then gets them all to go into the same garment. In the second, one designs a set of compatible modules and then keeps repeating them, each time inserting different colors from the color set.

Read and study the information on pushed neutrals in this chapter. Then use what you can, adapt what you can, or take the information a step further and invent something new. (Pushed-neutral color schemes adapt nicely to quilts, too.) As you read, keep in mind your skill level, body uniqueness, flamboyance quotient, and time commitment. Plan a project you can finish, finish a project you can wear, and wear a project you'll look great in.

WHAT IS A PUSHED-NEUTRAL COLOR SCHEME?

Since I invented the concept of a pushed-neutral color scheme, you can't read about it in other books on color. So what exactly is it?

Pushed neutrals are a new way to work with fabric and color in wearable art. If you have felt that decorative clothing was not for you because it was too showy, this color scheme is for you. Pushed neutrals are low contrast, calming and soothing to the eye and soul. Small-scale, all-over geometric pieced designs cover the surface with subtle color interest. You select a hue from anywhere on the color wheel that is pleasing to you, gray it, and combine it with beiges and grays. Here are some pushed-neutral color scheme possibilities:

> dusty rose to beige
> olive green to beige
> golden beige to gray
> gray-green to gray
> gray-blue to gray
> lavendar to gray

The Japanese word *shibui* could well be used to describe pushed-neutral garments. They are subtle.

COMPOSING A PUSHED-NEUTRAL COLOR SCHEME

While there is no magic number of colors to include in a pushed-neutral scheme, most quilters have to stretch to come up with eight. To create a vest, start by gathering together eight one-quarter-yard pieces of solid cotton or chintz.

Keep in mind that the most interesting effect occurs when the colors, beiges, and grays *don't* blend and there is a wide variety of mainly medium values. Learn to use both warms and cools. Warms are colors that have yellow in them. Cools are colors that move toward blue. For any color, there are both warm and cool versions. Learn to look for subtle variations. The differences are relative. Compare several samples and decide between them which is coolest and which is warmest.

More specifically, begin by deciding where on the color wheel you want to start. Make sure the color that you are pushing toward is grayed, *not* clear and bright. See if you can find three or four medium values of this color. It may be against your instincts, but it is important that the colors don't match perfectly. Pick both warm and cool versions of your color. If you prefer cool colors, a warm variation will add life. On the other hand, if you prefer warm colors, the cool version of your color will calm down your other choices a bit.

Next start looking at the solid beiges and grays at your fabric store or in your collection. You will be filling in with these fabrics. Eliminate clear colors; look for the duller versions. If you can't find any, too-clear colors can be over-dyed with Rit Dye. (Try tan or a tiny bit of black; unfortunately, Rit doesn't make a gray dye.)

You may find some colors that are right on the edge between being the hue you are working with and one of the neutrals. When you move the cloth bolts or pieces of fabric back and forth between the two sections, they appear to fit in either place. These are wonderful finds. Include them in your scheme.

It is most difficult to use the darkest and lightest values. Charcoal is okay if you have a higher flamboyance quotient, but black is way too dark. (Black and white are too bold and extreme to be subtle.) If you select gray to fill in, include a beige for variety. Use both warm and cool grays. If you select beige to fill in, include one gray for variety. Use both warm and cool beiges. Taupe is great because it has both gray and beige.

One advantage of having an extensive fabric collection is that you'll be able to find varied beiges and grays from past seasons to combine with what is currently on the market. In any given season, after awhile, the colors all seem to look alike—they have the same "temperature." Currently, cool grays and warm beiges predominate. Throwing in a cool beige or warm gray from a previous season will add a spark of life to an otherwise dull, "temperate" scheme. Hint: When you are auditioning candidates to add to your color scheme, place the fabric or bolt across all the other colors so you get a total feeling. Don't limit yourself to just comparing it with one or two of the colors.

This kind of color scheme often takes a lot of fine tuning. It's amazing how slight changes can make all the difference. And remember, there is no one right solution. I may think a scheme is fine, you may not. All of a sudden it will click! Rely on your intuition: listen to your inner voice.

Long ago I discovered this color scheme works best in solids. Some people assume that they can include calico prints. The only calicos that might possibly be candidates are the two-color ones. However, they tend to give an "oatmeal" effect: they "mush out" and look blah. Since the scheme is subtle to begin with, calicos usually detract rather than add to the total effect.

There are a few exceptions to the rule of no prints. Pin dots can hold their own. Some two-color geometric prints are also a welcome addition. See Pam Quan's vest "Softly Seminole" (Color Plates 9 and 10). If you love prints and can't bear a garment without them, use them for the lining.

A good way to check your color scheme before you actually commit yourself to making a vest is to do a glued mock-up. This allows you to see all the colors combined, plus gives an idea of how everything will look when pieced.

The exercise also eases you into working with a more subdued color scheme which at first may seem very foreign, particularly if you are used to making high-contrast quilts. Students in my series class often come back and tell me they like their scheme better and better each week. It grows on them.

Pushed-Neutral Mock-up

Here are directions for making a glued mock-up using eight colors (see Figure 2-1). You'll need eight fabrics (at least ¼ yard of each), a rotary cutter and mat (or scissors), a piece of white paper at least 8½" x 11", and a gluestick.

1. Open the fabric out flat and stack it. Across a short end, parallel to the selvage, cut off a 1" strip with your rotary cutter.
2. Next slice off four 1" squares from the strips.
3. Turn the four squares into triangles by cutting them in half diagonally.
4. You will now have eight stacks of triangles. *Stop:* Don't go any further until you have gone through your stacks and methodically arranged them by color.
5. Arrange your eight sets of eight triangles in a straight line in front of you. I usually put my main colors first and the neutral colors last. If two piles appear very similiar when stacked next to each other, rearrange their placement in the line before you begin. This will lessen the possibility of confusion later.
6. Beginning at the left side of the sheet of paper, put down a strip of glue. Pick up Color 1 and

Figure 2-1.
Cutting triangles for pushed-neutral mock-up.

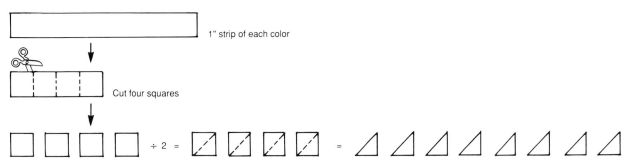

1" strip of each color

Cut four squares

$\div 2 =$ $=$

arrange the eight triangles in a vertical row on the glue. I normally arrange them so I separate the last one slightly away from the group at the bottom of the page. (Now all of Color 1 has been used.)

7. Next, select one triangle from *each* of the remaining piles to add to the row you have just put down. Beginning at the top, arrange them in descending order down your line of glue. (There won't be one for the triangle at the very bottom.) You have now tried Color 1 with all of the other seven choices.

8. Now go to the second pile. Staggering the beginning of your row one step, lay down the triangles from top to bottom, arranging them as you did in the first row. (Now all of Color 2 has been used.)

9. Repeat steps 7 and 8 until all your stacks of triangles are gone and your mock-up looks like Figure 2-2.

You should have a large right-angle triangle in which you have used each of your colors with all the other colors in your scheme. As a reminder of the specific colors in your scheme, you will have one row of single triangles across the bottom of the page.

Helpful hints to complete a successful exercise:

1. Though it's possible to fit the whole exercise on an 8½" x 11" piece of paper, a slightly larger piece gives a little extra room.

2. Don't use any other color paper except white or the color will interact and affect what you perceive.

3. I prefer to not have the triangles touch, so I can view each combination separately. To fit the bottom row of triangles on, however, you will have to let them touch.

4. Place and glue one row at a time. It is most efficient to lay down a strip of glue with your glue-stick before you begin each row.

5. We all handle a set of directions differently. If you are easily confused, select solitary peace and quiet to do this exercise.

6. If you get confused, throw out your triangles and re-read the directions. You will have enough fabric from your original strip to cut a second set of triangles.

After you have completed the exercise, evaluate the results. You will be surprised with some of your combinations. They may be color groupings you had never considered using together. This is also an opportunity for you to check your value contrast. If the large triangle looks too spotty to you, the finished garment will look the same way. There may be too wide a range in value.

Incidentally, Laura Munson Reinstatler enjoyed doing this exercise so much she repeated it on the bib of

Figure 2-2.
Pushed-neutral mock-up.

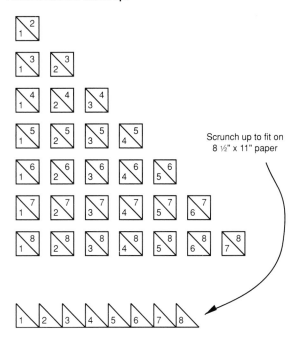

Scrunch up to fit on 8 ½" x 11" paper

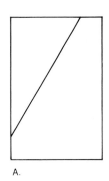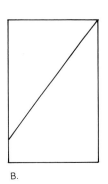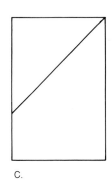

Figure 2-3.
Doodling exercise—one line.

1"

1½"

No!   A.   B.   C.

a wonderful, understated dress! (See Color Plates 11 and 12.)

It's possible to compose a pushed-neutral color scheme beginning anywhere on the color wheel. However, if you feel you need more direction in composing a possible scheme, just look around you. Here are some suggested sources for color ideas:

1. *Linens and decorator fabrics.*
    The Southwest Look—pushed neutral in feel—is still in.
2. *Nature.*
    For example, my "Eucalyptus" vest is based on a photo essay of eucalyptus trees in a local park.
3. *The environment around you.*
    a. House color. My area of the country provides many interesting schemes because all the houses aren't brick or painted white. Many Victorian homes have very elaborate color schemes that can be adapted.
    b. Paint chip cards from the paint or hardware store. These help train your eye to see subtle differences in color.
    c. I even found a beautiful pushed-neutral scheme in a window I had photographed at Paul Revere's house in Boston. I didn't realize it was there until I got home and looked at the developed photos.

Once you have a perceptual set to see pushed-neutral color schemes, you will see them everywhere. Often when I am out teaching, I have automatically noticed that the tile on the floor of the bathroom is a pushed-neutral color scheme. By noontime, my students are eager to inform me of this important fact!

Though it's fun to come up with a pushed-neutral color scheme for a garment, it's just as important to decide what you are going to wear with it to get a total effect. It doesn't have to be a runway ensemble either; a simple blouse or T-shirt and skirt or pants will do. Jumpsuits are also great.

Keep in mind your flamboyance quotient. If you are the understated sort and feel that pushed neutrals are for you, you are probably right. Be careful to limit the range of values in your garment. Don't go all the way from medium-lights to medium-darks. Make sure your other clothes help you carry off the feeling of your vest. Aim for a neutral effect where the vest blends into the total effect.

At the other end of the flamboyance spectrum, if you are a striking person with dramatic differences in your coloring, you may feel this scheme won't work for you. Try a wider range of contrast in your color values. Wear your vest with black clothing. A striking friend, Salle Crittenden, wore "Amtrak" in a fashion show with a black jumpsuit. It contrasted with the subtle scheme of the vest and made for a dramatic outfit. Even on me, the vest changes considerably when I change what I wear with it, as you can see in Color Plates 1 and 2. No garment is an island; everything we wear interacts with our other clothing and with our own coloring and style.

DESIGNING WITH REPETITIVE DESIGNS

There are many ways that the pushed-neutral color scheme could be presented in wearables. I've used two approaches in designing my garments—repetitive designs and a modular approach. It's a good idea to give

Figure 2-4.
Doodling exercise—two lines.

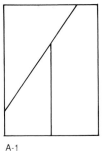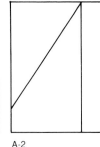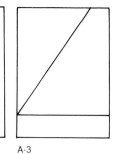

A-1   A-2   A-3

both a try to see which is the most comfortable for you. In this section, we consider designing with repetitive designs. Look at the color pictures of various pushed-neutral garments. Those that use the concept of repetitive designs are seen in Color Plates 1 through 3 and 7 through 10.

Doodling Exercises

The first set of exercises works best on graph paper with eight squares per inch. (You will also want a small ruler and a sharp pencil with an eraser.) This size graph paper makes the enlarging exercise a little easier to do. If you can't find paper with eight squares per inch, though, just use the kind with four squares per inch.

Getting Started Exercise

1. Draw ten unattached rectangles, each 1" x 1½" (Figure 2-3).
2. Divide each rectangle in a different way. Limit yourself to one or two nonintersecting, straight lines for each.
3. Pick your most interesting rectangle and use it in the following exercises.

This exercise shows how easy it is to create some interesting divisions of space. When selecting your best design, eliminate any that divide the space evenly or in an obvious way. An example of an obvious division would be a line drawn diagonally from corner to corner to form two triangles. More interesting diagonal divisions are seen in Rectangles A, B, or C in Figure 2-3.

Though only one dividing line was used in the example, a second line could also be added. Add one to rectangle A (Figure 2-4), and see how the design changes. The doodles are often the most interesting when at least one of the lines drawn is a diagonal.

Once you have designed some pleasing doodles, it is important to see how they will look when they are repeated in rows since this is the way you would use them in your garment.

Letter "L" Exercise

1. Assemble five connected rectangles to create a large "L" (Figure 2-5). The dimensions are:
$$\text{top} = 1"$$
$$\text{vertical side} = 4½"$$
$$\text{base} = 3"$$
2. Draw the rectangle you selected in the first exercise in the five new rectangles that form the "L."
3. Shade in the separate parts of each rectangle in the same way. If there are three segments, use crosshatching or dots. Colored pencils are fine, too.

Figure 2-5.
Letter "L" exercise.

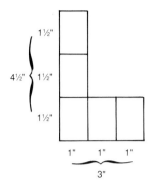

Figure 2-6.
Evaluation of "L" exercise. Look at both the vertical and horizontal possibilities.

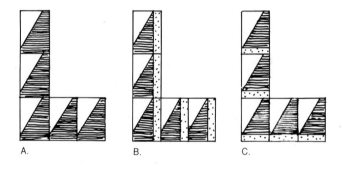

A.   B.   C.

Figure 2-7.
Rectangles placed on their sides.

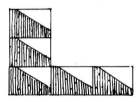

Figure 2-8.
Rotating rectangle placement.

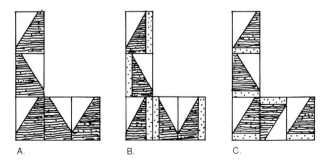

A.   B.   C.

This exercise shows how the units will look when they are connected vertically and horizontally. Let's evaluate the rectangles in Figure 2-6.

1. Rectangle A looks good vertically and horizontally.
2. Rectangle B looks good horizontally. Vertically, the same effect could have been achieved by adding a long strip along one edge, rather than adding the same small strip three times. Don't take the time to do complicated piecing if it won't show.
3. Rectangle C looks good vertically. Horizontally, it has the same problems as B does vertically.

Repeat this exercise, but arrange the rectangles on their side instead (Figure 2-7). Also, try rotating alternate blocks in the vertical and horizontal lines, as shown in Figure 2-8. The more you experiment, the more fun it is.

Enlarging Exercise

You probably wouldn't enjoy sewing these doodle-sized rectangles. Some of us might have the skill to do it, but for many, it would be pure frustration. Now that you have a stockpile of possible designs, let's enlarge them to a size that you *could* sew comfortably.

1. Using graph paper, draw a rectangle twice as large as your original one, that is, 2" x 3".
2. Transfer your dividing line or lines to this enlarged rectangle (Figure 2-9).
3. Evaluate this new, larger rectangle. Do you have the skill level to sew it? How is it scaled to your body size?

You may find the larger rectangle is easier to sew, but it may be a bit more bold than you would wish when repeated in a series across your body. If the rectangle was too large, try this:

1. Using graph paper, draw a rectangle one-and-a-half times as large as your original one. The measurement would be 1½" x 2¼".
2. Transfer your dividing line or lines to the new rectangle (Figure 2-10).

Most people are more pleased with this second, smaller enlargement. Then why didn't I just have you use it to begin with? Because this exercise shows you the process involved in enlarging doodles.

We have been doodling with small rectangles, but you could also doodle with squares or triangles. What you are looking for is simple geometric shapes that can be joined to create strips.

Figure 2-9.
Enlarging two times.

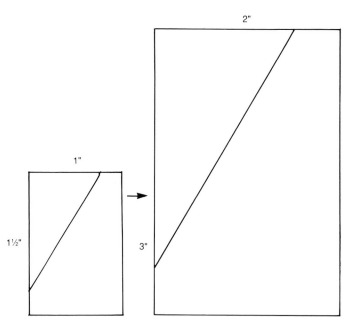

Figure 2-10.
Enlarging one-and-a-half times.

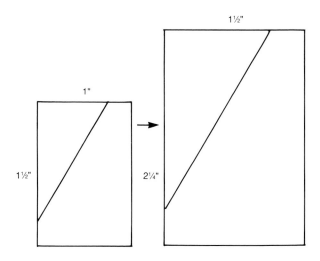

Your doodling will help you learn to look for appropriate designs in the environment around you. I have photographed floor tiles and jotted down knit sweater designs. Look through your quilt books. Often entire blocks or borders, or parts of them, can be used. Have a perceptual set to see pieced designs, and you'll see them everywhere.

Carry a small notebook to jot down ideas, notes, or sketches of what you see. These experiences are fleeting; capture them when they happen. Don't feel embarrassed about taking out your notebook to make notes.

Most people are impressed by your awareness level, and will take you more seriously. Even if you never read the note again, the act of making it intensifies the moment and helps you focus on what you are really seeing.

Major and Minor Design Areas

When you look at your design ideas, and translate them visually into body-sized garment pieces, you may decide that there's an awful lot of space to fill. If you become overwhelmed and fear you will never finish, consider this: all the parts don't have to be equally interesting or complex to piece. I like working with the idea of major and minor design areas.

By definition, a major area is important, it is bolder, it makes a statement. On the other hand, a minor area is less important, but supportive. The major area may have more complicated piecing; the minor, something that can be done quickly with speed techniques. The major area may also make more of a color statement; the minor one, a supportive but noncompetitive one.

My "Amtrak-Am-Slow" vest (Color Plates 1 through 3) is a good example. I began with an asymmetrically designed pattern front so it was easy to declare the overlapping side more important than the one that was tucked under. The major front is divided into two areas. Displayed center front is a set of elongated triangles drafted into a curved edge. Silver buttons held in place with loop closures help to emphasize the shaped edge and call attention to the precision piecing. On the other side of the elongated triangles, several narrow strips and a row of pieced blocks run vertically and act as a divider. The second area has horizontal piecing joined together with strips of varying width and color. It is finished off top and bottom with strip piecing.

The minor front is almost totally made up of the narrow strip piecing which was used to complete the major front. The strips run vertically and are broken in the upper area by several bands of staggered strips surrounding a row of pieced blocks.

The major front took many hours to complete; the minor one, very little time. However, it is still an important part of the garment. The simplicity of its piecing acts as a foil for the more complicated piecing on the other front. Only six colors appear on the minor front; ten on the other. The addition of the warmer colors to the major front help to emphasize its importance. However, there is sufficient repetition of color to marry the two sides.

Creating Filler: Strip Piecing and Tucking

Filler is uncomplicated and simple, but it performs an important function in some wearables because it occupies space that needs to be filled with something other than plain fabric or complicated piecing. Creating filler speeds up the garment completion time because it is relatively easy and quick to do. Here are some ideas for making filler:

a. *Even Stripping.* Strip piecing has been used to get fast results for years. Some of us are bored to tears of seeing it used in quilted wearables because it looks so elementary. It is more interesting in "Amtrak" because the strips are narrow, only ¾" wide. It is scaled to the size of the small pieced blocks.

b. *Unplanned Random Stripping.* Another way to generate some fast filler with strip piecing is to vary the width of the strips used in a random way (see Figure 2-11). You may actually have exactly the same number of strips and be able to cover the same area, but it looks more complicated and sophisticated.

c. *Planned Uneven Stripping.* D'Ova Siemers used strip piecing as filler in still a third way (see Photo 6). I call it planned uneven stripping (Figure 2-12). She has combined a very narrow strip with a wider one and repeated them to create a simple pattern. The color is varied in the narrow strips but remains constant in the wider ones.

d. *Planned Uneven Stripping with Cording.* If you enjoy doing cording, you could adapt planned uneven stripping by inserting corded strips where D'Ova has

Figure 2-11.
Unplanned random stripping.

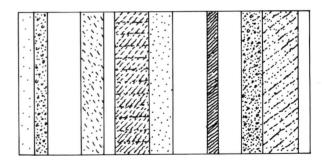

Figure 2-12.
Planned uneven stripping.

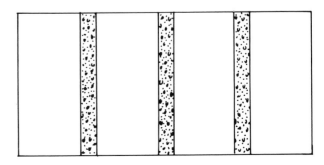

used her narrow strips. Increase the width of the wider strips to facilitate pressing. This method works best on garments that will be drycleaned.

e. *Tucking.* I have always loved garments with tucking and have often included it in my wearable garments (and quilts). Tucking adds surface interest, but still remains subtle and understated. The stitching can be done in the same or contrasting thread. See Figure 2-16, and the accompanying discussion, for more details on tucking.

DESIGNING WITH A MODULAR APPROACH

As mentioned earlier, I have worked primarily with two approaches to using pushed neutrals in garments, repetitive designs and modules. Now let's take a look at this second approach.

While many people feel totally comfortable with generating a series of repetitive designs, for some it is pure torture to figure out what to do with them once they exist. It's a huge step from making strips to actually putting them in place. If this sounds like you, take heart—modules may be your answer. Once you have the designs for a set of modules, you just make them until there are enough to fill the required space. This approach is also good for larger-busted women who would rather create an all-over feeling in their garments where the eye moves continuously. To keep the eye moving, minimize value contrast. Eliminate any of the too light or too dark colors that stand out too much.

If you can only work on your projects in snatches of time, the modular approach is ideal. Once you have created the designs for the modules, the project can be done piecemeal and you won't feel too disjointed. Compose a module while dinner is cooking, then stitch it together after the dishes are done or the kids tucked in.

You also may enjoy using this approach just to try something new. It's an opportunity to stretch your creativity, to use parts of your brain you may not have been using. Understand that any discomfort you experience is probably only temporary.

Doodling Exercise

You will need a sharp pencil, an eraser, graph paper (four squares per inch), and a small ruler for this exercise.

1. Draw a series of six unattached rectangles, each 3" x 5".
2. Divide the space in each rectangle in a different way, using straight lines.
3. There is *no* limit to the number of lines that can be used, but remember each line represents a seam, so keep in mind the following things about yourself:
   a. Skill level—you will have to sew it this size.
   b. Body size—the pieces must relate to you in scale. (Small women particularly need to consider this one; large women may prefer to start with a 4" x 6" rectangle.)
   c. Time commitment—plan something you have a hope of finishing.

Having analyzed many sets of rectangles produced in workshops, I've discovered if you draw enough (probably more than six) the rectangles become distinctive in style. It's a little like your personal handwriting. You may not be aware of this unless you compare your work to someone else's. Sometimes, even in one's own doodles, several styles will emerge.

It is important to generate enough rectangles that match in feeling to give a unified effect to your garment. Five or six are probably all you need. Figure 2-13 shows the set of modules I used for "Eucalyptus." This set of modules has a "quilterly" feeling to them. They are very predictable because they look like quilt blocks.

Figure 2-13.
"Eucalyptus" modules.

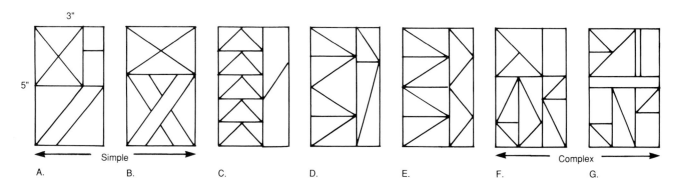

Simple →   ← Complex

A.   B.   C.   D.   E.   F.   G.

Figure 2-14.
Rejected "Eucalyptus" modules.

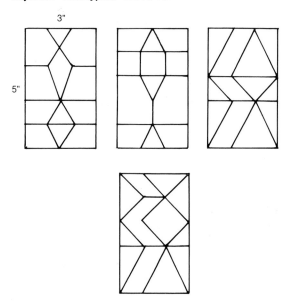

Look at four of the modules I rejected from my original batch (Figure 2-14). They have the feeling of another handwriting. They don't look quite so quilterly. The division of space isn't as regimented and predictable; they are moving toward an abstract feeling. If I doodled some more, I could extend this set.

Months later, I did draw another set of modules. This time as a requirement, I said that they *had* to be abstract. I added another limitation and got what I wanted.

Composing a Module

After you have selected the modules you will use, make your templates. Refer to the section on drafting in Chapter 6 if you need help. When you are working on a small scale, precision is even more important.

There are several ways to approach color selection and arrangement in your modules. When working on "Eucalyptus," I found that I could manage two blocks at once. In fact, when I was working on module A, I discovered I could handle four blocks at once. I stacked my fabrics in a pile on the table. As I composed a block, I went through the pile. It's important to use all the colors. The tendency is to have favorites which you keep being drawn to while there are others that you forget to use. Be fair and give equal attention to all.

I cut out and stitched my blocks, using tandem piecing, before going on to compose another set. I found it more efficient to sew several sets of the same block because I got into the swing of things from repeating the same steps in the same order.

When I started a new block of the same module, I kept its "sisters" on the table in front of me. In this way, I could check to make sure I wasn't creating duplicates.

As individual parts were stitched together, I kept checking them against my original drawing to ensure that I wasn't getting off track.

When I work, I use some speed techniques, but I often have to force myself to remember them, just as I have to remember to use my food processor. All too easily I can get into the "zen" of tracing and hand cutting. It's very relaxing to me; it also takes a long time.

When the modular approach was presented to Dorothy Clarke, she decided to speed things up a bit for "Urban Lilacs." (See Color Plates 13 and 14.) After making her templates, she piled up her fabrics and stack-cut sets of each template with her rotary cutter. This probably took the same amount of time as it did for me to trace and cut one triangle out of one piece of fabric! When Dorothy got ready to compose she had little piles of each piece cut in many colors sitting in front of her. She could make as many modules as she had colors...probably eight at a time.

A word of warning. Make an effort to keep your piles separated. Use baggies, custard cups, muffin pans, etc. This is particularly important when you work in scattered pieces of time, or if others, including pets, have access to your workspace.

There are other ways that the process of using modules can be speeded up. For Paulie Carlson's Art Nouveau series (Photos 1 through 3), she drew simpler blocks but cut some of the pieces out of "manufactured" fabric so the all-over effect was equally complicated. For the fabric, she created "half-square" or "sheeted" triangles, random-pieced strips, and tucking.

Strategies for Using Modules

As I sewed my "Eucalyptus" modules, I discovered that some took longer to complete than others. In fact, module G was so time-consuming that I sewed it up once just to prove I could do it, placed it in an obvious center front position, and never attempted it again.

If some of the modules are easier for you, use more of them. There is no rule that says there has to be the same number of each type of module present. If you keep rotating your colors, and your blocks all have a similar feel, it's difficult for the viewer to keep track of what is going on. No one has ever come up to me when I was wearing "Eucalyptus" and told me I had more of module A than of the others.

It will take approximately 30 to 36 modules to completely fill an average vest, depending on your size and the fullness of the garment. You can estimate the number of modules needed by using one to "pace off" the area on each piece. Most likely you will end up needing some partial modules. Sometimes one can be split and used in several places. Sacrifice your least favorite ones for this.

**Photo 1. Art Nouveau I (detail).
Paulie Carlson, Houston, TX**

**Photo 2. Art Nouveau II.
Paulie Carlson, Houston, TX**

**Photo 3. Art Nouveau II (detail).
Paulie Carlson, Houston, TX**

To better fill the available space in "Eucalyptus," I placed some of the modules vertically and some horizontally. There is no set formula. This, however, is a good example of a "grid" as far as sewing the pieces together is concerned. Refer to the section on creating all-over grids in Chapter 6 if you are unsure of how to sew your modules together.

If the idea of filling a whole garment with modules overwhelms you, thumb through the color photographs and adapt something you see there. Possible choices might be major-minor design area ideas, filled in with quick stripping, or a strip two to three blocks wide placed diagonally on a plain or simple field.

You could also:

a. Decorate a panel with modules and make the rest of the garment from another fabric as Marjie Scharff did for her "Workshop Work-outfit," a casual outfit using sweatshirt fabric. (See Photo 4.) She machine quilted through batting, but you can also machine quilt through sweatshirt fabric.

b. Piece the front and leave the back plain. If you do this, it is important to give weight to the back so the garment won't always be pulling forward. Add batting and lining and hand or machine quilt the back.

c. Use the alternate block method used in quilts and leave every other block plain. I would suggest using your favorite medium-value fabric. Quilt each plain block the same way. The effect will be more spotty than an all-over pieced grid.

**Photo 4. Workshop Work-outfit.
Marjie Scharff, San Antonio, TX**

OTHER APPROACHES TO DESIGNING

I have presented two approaches to designing garments using the pushed-neutral color scheme—repetitive designs and a modular approach. There are other ways the color scheme could be used. Maybe some of these will appeal to you.

Figure 2-15.
Marion Ongerth modules.

Appliqué Modules

If appliqué is your thing, here's a very portable project idea (see Figure 2-15). Instead of piecing modules, hand appliqué them. This idea came to me when I saw a set of squares Marion Ongerth had done to practice her hand-appliqué stitch. I suggested cutting the squares into rectangles, a more slimming design if used in a garment.

Modular Sampler

D'Ova Siemers combined a variety of patchwork and fabric manipulation technique samples in the bodice of a beautiful back-wrapping dress, "Seattle Blues." An important design feature of the dress, shown in Photos 5 and 6, was an additional diagonal piece that cut across the front, tapering to an end on the back. To accentuate this feature, she gave it a contrasting, darker value by selecting to emphasize the darker colors in her collection. When creating filler fabric for the back, she sewed very narrow strips from her fabrics with wider strips of her major color, pale blue. This is an example of planned uneven stripping. (See Figure 2-12.) Notice how the stripping has been lined up with the patched grid above so the two are beautifully integrated. D'Ova's piecing gives the same effect that cording would, but since the surface is relatively flat, pressing is simplified.

Photo 5. Seattle Blues (front).
D'Ova Siemers, Kirkland, WA

Photo 6. Seattle Blues (back).
D'Ova Siemers, Kirkland, WA

Photo 7. New Beginnings. Marian Etzler, Kirkland, WA

Marian Etzler, a student of D'Ova's, arranged her samples on the front of a slip-over top, "New Beginnings," which was banded with crochet (Photo 7). The back was solid and made from a woven, suede-like fabric. She selected neutral beige to wear with her handsome top.

Seminole Patchwork

Thanks to Cheryl Bradkin and Lassie Wittman, quilters have been using Seminole patchwork for years. If you are familiar with this technique, you might enjoy using it in a garment with a pushed-neutral color scheme.

Watching my students, I noticed their difficulty in getting a unified feeling when combining Seminole with traditional piecing. I think Pam Quan has conquered the problem in her piece, "Softly Seminole." (See Color Plates 9 and 10.) One of the reasons she succeeded is her clever use of triangular clusters of her design segments; these complement the diagonals found in the Seminole piecing and in the triangles. Notice these clusters on the left side of the front and back of the garment.

She has also included print fabric. Though two-color calicos generally don't make enough of a statement, her geometric print works wonderfully because it's bold enough to hold its own. Her second print is a very small circle that reads like a pin dot.

Accent

Here is an idea from Laura Munson Reinstatler for using just an accent of a pushed-neutral scheme. Vowing to create an understated, very wearable garment, Laura used woven self-fabric strips of her corduroy vest fabric to embellish "March Winds" (Photo 8). To add a touch of sparkle to the front and back, she added three strips of the meticulously perfect ¼" stripping she is known for nationally. Her pushed-neutral scheme contains 14 colors in addition to the basic gray. Laura can design for the runway, but she also creates comfortable garments for more casual settings.

TECHNICAL ADVICE FOR PUSHED NEUTRALS

The small-scale piecing used in making the garments in this chapter requires accuracy, and that means each step along the way must be accurate. You should be able to:

1. Draft patterns accurately.
2. Make templates accurately, including adding a seam allowance.
3. Cut out individual pieces accurately, whether by individually tracing and cutting or by using speed techniques.
4. Sew blocks accurately, taking a ¼" seam allowance.

Many beginning quilters are a bit casual in their approach to accuracy; for them, speed is the thing.

Photo 8. March Winds. Laura Munson Reinstatler, Mill Creek, WA

Beginners intent on churning out as much as possible in as short a time as possible may find it easier to use fewer, larger pieces rather than more, smaller pieces. Just keep your body size in mind and don't make the pieces too big. If your skill level right now keeps you from doing all the things you want to, work on improving it. Accuracy can be learned and it must be practiced. If you feel you'd like to improve your accuracy, read about precision techniques in Chapter 6.

Hand and Machine Quilting

If you can't decide how to quilt your pushed-neutral garment, read the section on quilting in Chapter 6 for some helpful tips. Here are two ideas to get you started.

Repetitive Segments

If you decide to hand quilt your pushed-neutral garment, you will have to determine how much quilting to use. Although it isn't necessary to quilt every line, it's best and safest to have *some* quilting when there are so many small pieces.

Look at Color Plates 1 through 3. The majority of the very tiny pieces were not quilted because of their size. I did quilt some of the strips connecting these segments, however. The longest stretch without hand quilting was 4¼" and most was much closer. There is a lot of quilting in the stripping areas. I used several plain strips on the back which were embellished with geometric patterns done in quilting. In both cases, there is more than the minimum quilting necessary; I was having a good time!

To highlight the long shaped triangles at center front, I quilted close to the seam lines. I was careful about the direction I was pressing the seams as I didn't want to quilt through them. The amount of quilting in "Amtrak" seems adequate. It's held up well through repeated wearings and drycleanings.

Modules

If you are overwhelmed with the thought of hand quilting your modules, consider machine quilting your grids. However, if you also enjoy hand quilting, you might like to take a closer look at Color Plate 5. The quilting has a more contemporary look and feel to it. Here's the procedure for hand quilting modules:

1. As modules are created, press the seams. Don't worry about which direction to press them, nor do you need to press matching modules in the same way.
2. Construct your fabric from the modules.
3. Quilt block by block, remembering if there *is* a seam allowance, stitch next to it; if there is *no* seam allowance, stitch next to the seam line.

What I especially like about this method is that it is irregular and haphazard. Some geometric shapes are outlined with quilting ¼" from the seam line, a few have quilting only next to the seam line, and many shapes are outlined with a combination of the two techniques.

To mark the lines, I use ¼" masking tape laid over the seam allowance. You may prefer to just feel the ridge left by the seam, or to mark your seam in whatever manner you're accustomed to using. I like to use tape because it is straight, easy to apply, and easy to remove, at least if done right after I finish quilting. Otherwise, it gets sticky and leaves a residue.

EMBELLISHMENTS

Piecing, appliqué, and quilting lines add surface interest to a garment. You might also consider using some form of embellishment to further enrich the surface.

Tucks

Tucking is ideal for pushed-neutral garments because it is so subtle, so versatile, and so easy. Tucking can be stitched in matching or contrasting thread, it can be used alone as a filler for a minor area, or in strips as filler between pieced areas. It can also be incorporated into pieced blocks. For two innovative uses of tucking, look at the garments by Paulie Carlson and Dorothy Clarke. In Photo 3, Paulie tucked pieces of fabric and then cut

Figure 2-16.
Tuck variations.

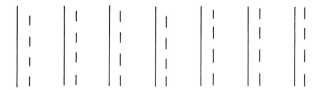

A. Even tucks, even spacing.

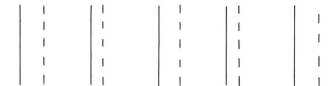

B. Uneven tucks, even spacing.

C. Even tucks, uneven spacing.

Figure 2-17.
Marking and sewing tucks.

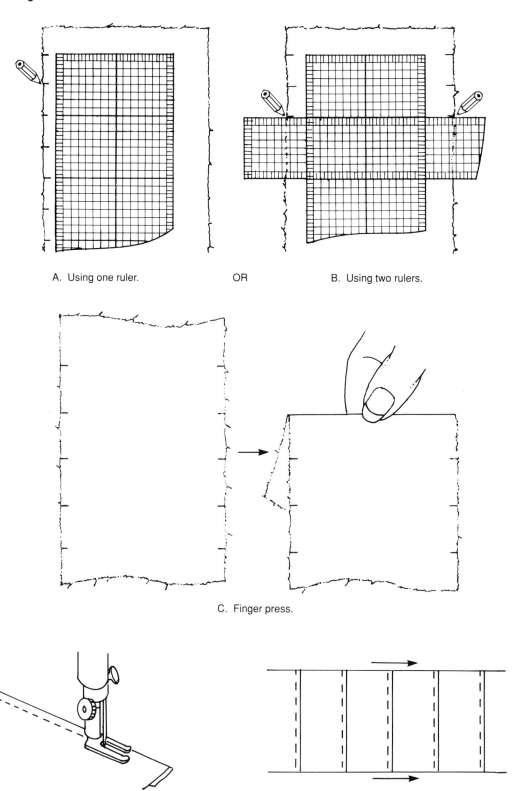

A. Using one ruler.   OR   B. Using two rulers.

C. Finger press.

D. Stitch.   E. Press all tucks in same direction.

individual pattern pieces using a template. In Color Plate 8, Dorothy ran individual tucks across pieces of fabric and then positioned her templates randomly so an occasional line would be included when she cut her fabric.

For tucking to look good, individual folds must be consistent in width and must be stitched straight. The actual size of a progression of tucks can vary as long as you establish a pattern and keep to it. To get started, look at the three possible repeated tuck variations in Figure 2-16. It's quite easy to do repetitive tucks on your sewing machine (Figure 2-17):

1. Cut the fabric to be tucked. I often use 4" wide strips that are 6" to 18" long.
2. Using a See-thru ruler, mark off the two corresponding edges with small pencil marks at the edges. To mark both edges at the same time, position a second smaller ruler perpendicularly across the larger ruler.
3. With your thumbnail, crease a fold line between corresponding marks. For narrow widths, pressing is unnecessary, though it may be helpful for wider areas.
4. Stitch the tucks, using your presser foot as a guide for a consistent width. (On my Singer Featherweight machine, which has a foot with a large and small toe, I use the small toe as a guide. I also don't backstitch, but use a slightly smaller stitch instead.)
5. Stitch all the tucks before pressing the entire strip in one motion.

Leaves

I invented the leaves for my "Eucalyptus" vest when I had to come up with a front embellishment in one evening. (See Color Plate 6.) Though I'd been trying to figure out what to do for some time, an impending photography date provided the impetus to find a fast solution.

I ended up tracing around some real eucalyptus leaves leftover from my original color study. I then stacked several layers of fabric and stitched around the pencil outlines, then down the centers to look like veins. I left all the threads hanging so there would be a way to tie on my leaves. Then I cut out the individual leaves, cutting close to the stitched edges.

Some of the leaves curl because I asked, "What would happen if I used bias for one of the layers?" With the addition of antique Chinese buttons that were remarkably similiar to real pods, and the hanging threads, my leaves ended up looking quite realistic. Many leaves could be treated in a similar way and used as embellishment on garments.

Buttons

Besides the antique metal buttons I used on "Eucalyptus," I've also used old coins for embellishment. In Color Plate 3, I used the buffalo side of Indian head nickels for buttons. (No, it's not illegal to so treat American coins, as long as you don't try to pass them off as money!) Maybe you have old or foreign coins you could turn into buttons.

I used self-fabric loops to fasten the buttons. These are narrow bias strips that are folded in half lengthwise, seamed along one edge, turned with a loop turner, shaped into a loop, and then stitched into place. Making loops is easier than trying to put buttonholes in quilted fabric. Laura Munson Reinstatler did away with buttons and buttonholes altogether and used fabric ties for her understated corduroy vest, shown in Photo 8.

3

HAND-DYED FABRIC

With all the fabric on the market, why dye your own or use fabric dyed by real people as opposed to fabric made in a commercial factory? With commercially produced fabric, you are limited by the range of colors currently popular or the colors that your quilt store decides to stock. You may not be able to find just the color you want, or the value you had in mind. For some quilters, hand-dyed fabrics provide one more way to have control of the design process.

I first used hand-dyed fabric in 1983. My sister was teaching stained-glass quilting technique in Japan and I persuaded her to let me have the remains of her class swatches. I was possessed with this beautiful fabric dyed by Akio Kawamota and had to turn it into a vest. The result, seen in Color Plate 18, is "Midnight Rainbow," a simple vest using flowing, curved strings of wedge-shaped pieces of fabric across a field of black chintz. If you look closely at the pink lining, you may be able to see that the surface of the fabric is not just one flat value. I love this special effect and have used Mr. Kawamota's fabric in a number of my story quilts.

Several years later, I took a wonderful workshop from Debra Millard Lunn in which members of my quilting guild spent an entire day stirring dye pots. At the end of the day, we each took home little stacks of some of the most beautiful pieces of muslin I have ever seen. I couldn't wait to use this fabric; I also realized I would never stir a dye pot again. However, that long day did give me an appreciation of the process involved in hand-dyeing fabric. I made a quilt from my samples, and then I used the leftover scraps to create "Daydreams," shown in Color Plates 19 and 20.

Some of the garments shown in the color photographs are made with fabric actually dyed by their makers; other garments were made from fabric dyed by others. If you are interested in trying the process, Debra Millard Lunn's book on fabric dyeing is an excellent resource. You can also purchase hand-dyed fabric. If your local quilt store doesn't carry it, try one of the mail-order sources listed in the Appendix.

Theoretically, it would be possible to have any color you wanted if you dyed it yourself and possessed the expertise to know just how much of what needed to be added to your dyeing solution. For most of us, though, we are at the mercy of the hand-dyers, much as we are with the makers of commercially produced fabric. They dye their personal favorites or the colors they feel will sell. Happily, while not providing an unlimited range of fabric colors, the hand-dyers of today do produce a creative, marvelous alternative to factory fabrics.

Some hand-dyed fabric has a beautiful depth of color, a rich suede-like appearance that is mysteriously compelling. Often the surface is not just one flat color, but contains small streaks or areas of darker or lighter coloration.

HAND-DYED FABRIC AND ITS USE

There are many ways to hand-dye fabric. Often a group of fabric is dyed in some sort of progression. The three most common progressions are dyeing from one end of the rainbow to the other, dyeing a number of values of one hue, or dyeing from one color on the color wheel to a second color featuring intermediate steps along the way. It is possible to use any of these groupings in making wearables.

Polychromatic

My first two hand-dyed fabric garments used polychromatic, or rainbow, progressions. If you have taken a class in hand-dyeing you probably have a stack of rainbow fabrics, too. In the class with Debra Millard Lunn, we dyed the color spectrum in 28 steps. The tendency in using this type of fabric is to arrange them in their natural color order, or progression, because it feels so comfortable and looks natural to the eye.

Thank goodness I like small-scale piecing because I was indeed working with small pieces of fabric when I created "Daydreams," one of my first garments using hand-dyed fabrics. (See Color Photos 19 and 20.) There was insufficient fabric for an entire garment, so straight away I knew I would have to use something else—I settled on my navy chintz scraps. For surface interest, I tucked the chintz in strips. As I worked across the back of the vest, I realized I was running out of this fabric as well and wouldn't have enough to complete the second front!

It's uncomfortable to keep running out of fabric when trying to complete a project, but this kind of dilemma forces me to be more creative. Since I had been using scraps of hand-dyed fabric and chintz from one of my quilts, I decided to incorporate the one print that I had also used in the quilt. It was a wonderful Liberty of London cloud fabric. I used it on the garment back, one front, and on the collar, that is, repeating it in three of the four main areas. Remember, repetition of fabrics and colors helps tie the parts together.

My garment design was loosely based on the kimono style. Since the fronts are overlapping, I can lap the right over the left or vice versa. It's interesting to compare the two possibilities. In Color Plate 19, the garment is wrapped in the traditional Western, "female" way, that is, right over left. (In the photos, this appears to be just the opposite; however, overlapping is defined from the viewpoint of the person wearing the garment.) This was the first front constructed. It's nice, but nothing to write home about.

In Color Plate 20, with a left-over-right overlap, the second front is featured. Of necessity, I had to stretch myself here and the result is far more interesting and exciting. It really has become the major front designwise, and the other, first, front has become the minor one.

Gradations

Gradations were the first type of hand-dyed fabric available for purchase. Most of this fabric is dyed in eight steps and it's possible to create illusions of depth by sequencing the steps. This is fine for optical quilts, but not for wearables where we need to relate the design to the human body. Three garments that successfully use gradations appear in the color photographs (see Color Plates 21, 22, and 28).

Roz Zinns chose to make a long jacket with gradations, shown in Color Plate 21. The collar, back yoke,

and cuffs have been pieced, but the remainder of the garment has only a corded trim to highlight the cut of the pattern pieces. Vast areas of black help to dilute the impact of the pieced cording. Worn with black slacks, the jacket is fairly understated.

Dorothy Clarke sequences her gradations in tucks on the asymmetrical front and center back of her "Ripples" suit in Color Plate 22. Dorothy is petite and knew when to stop. Using plain denim for the rest of the jacket and the plain skirt helps her carry off the three-dimensional tucks. (If you would like to know how to do these tucks, try Lois Ericson's book, *Fabrics...Reconstructed: A Collection of Surface Changes*.)

"Route 66" was the first garment I made with hand-dyed gradations. (See Color Plate 28 and the detailed view in Color Plate 29.) I created a checkerboard effect for the jacket bodice by alternating pieced blocks with "puff" squares.

Having so many color gradations available was initially thrilling, but after just one project, most of us find we need to combine these fabrics with something else—alone they can easily appear too mechanical and perfect. Some people feel hand-dyed fabrics lack life and vitality when used by themselves. Such fabrics are not as simple to use as originally assumed.

Another problem with color gradations is that the difference between steps is very slight when there are eight steps from dark to light; in fact, in some colors it's almost impossible to see the difference when comparing steps right next to each other. Try dividing your fabric into two groupings rather than eight gradations. To do this, spread out the gradation so that you can see all eight steps. In the first pile, place pieces 1, 3, 5, and 7. In the second, place pieces 2, 4, 6, and 8. By skipping a step, the gradation differences are easier to discern. Now you have only four steps in your final color gradation, but essentially you have twice as much fabric to use since the two groupings look almost exactly alike (see Photo 9).

Still another difficulty with hand-dyed gradations is that the value contrast is too great from one end to the other of the color gradation. That can create a spotty

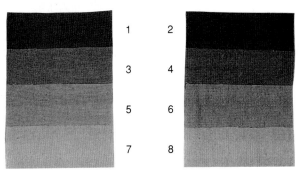

A. 8-step gradation.

B. Gradation regrouped into two similar sets of four steps.

Photo 9. Grouping gradations for use.

Photo 10. Western Roses. Carol Ann Wadley, Hillsboro, OR

surface if you use all eight of your colors in one garment. You may find it easier to remove the shades or tints at one of the ends. Carol Ann Wadley's vest, "Western Roses" (Photo 10) shows that removing the lighter tints made the color gradation easier to coordinate with the rose floral print. Carol Ann wanted a very wearable garment; by reducing the value contrast, the finished garment became more understated. Leftovers can be used for the lining or saved for another project. Also note the difference in the values of the denim used, achieved by using the right *and* wrongs sides of Carol Ann's fabric. You could also use Rit "Fast Fade for Jeans," a concentrated pre-wash, to lighten part of your fabric.

Dyeing from One Color to Another

Another way to hand-dye fabric is to select two colors on the color wheel and then dye steps to progress between the two. The individual steps can also be done in gradations while you're at it. Debra Millard Lunn did this for her vest, "Moonbow Confetti," which was part of an ensemble for the Fairfield Fashion Show. (See Color Plate 15.) Her beginning colors were orange and green. She cut her fabric into small squares, then randomly pieced them back together to form a grid pattern which was streaked diagonally across the vest front. Note that the colors were randomly placed not only by color but by value. She has also featured some of the fabric in random-sized strips that fill the minor areas.

Ann Verhoeven selected a similar color scheme when dyeing the 12 fabric colors for "A Sleeve Short and Feeling Foolish," shown in Color Plate 16. She presented her fabric in a grid of triangles and squares. To add interest and texture to the composition, she added a print fabric made into puffs. She also stacked and slashed some squares. White denim was dyed in one of the colors and used for the sleeves, back, and other unpieced areas.

My garment, "Sunset: Coast Highway One," is made from fabric hand-dyed by Stacy Michell. (See Color Plates 24 and 25.) Her beginning colors were pink and blue. She dyed in six steps, passing through purple. I have created another grid pattern alternating origami puffs with one of Stacy's "drop cloths," a fabric with color randomly brushed on. This fabric was also used to make a matching blouse. The jacket sleeves and pedal pushers were made from my mom's old chenille bedspread. (The one we were never allowed to sit on once the bed was made!)

Combining Dyeing and Painting

Once quilters get involved with dyeing fabric, they often take the next step and start painting fabric, too. Salle Crittenden, who particularly enjoys painting on fabric, embellished the fabrics in "Oklahoma Crude" (Color Plates 26 and 27). She used a variety of luxury fabrics and didn't worry as she streaked her paints onto them. Some of the paints were pearlized which added another dimension to the fabrics. Later the fabrics could be cut into squares, folded into puffs, and tucked with silver thread. Salle's jacket, a sampler of fabrics and painting techniques brought together by a common color scheme, is a prime example of the "what would happen if" principle.

We have now seen three outfits using the same Vogue Carol Horn pattern. (Unfortunately, the pattern is discontinued.) Salle's "Oklahoma Crude," and my "Route 66" and "Sunset: Coast Highway One," all provide a good opportunity to see just how different individual interpretations can be. Salle, a dramatic, striking woman, selected a similarly dramatic black-and-white scheme with red accents. In a similar outfit, I also used black denim, but teamed it with a turquoise gradation. For my glitter, I used silver buttons and studs for trim. (I consider myself animated rather than dramatic, with a red head's coloring.) My other outfit from the same pattern is more playful, with softer colors and fabric; the chenille sleeves and pedal pushers add a touch of memories.

Adding Other Fabrics

Once you begin to experiment with hand-dyed fabric, you may experience an urge to combine it with other fabrics rather than just using it by itself. However, it's not always easy to decide what will go with hand-dyed fabric. If you're looking for solids to expand your available collection, chintz and denim work well as filler because they present a decidedly different texture. Check the variety of ways both chintz and denim are used in the outfits in the color photographs.

You also may want to mix your gradations with other fabrics as they are being pieced or appliquéd. Look at Color Plate 32 to see Dorothy Clarke's second hand-dyed outfit, "Leaves in a Gentle Breeze." She selected a turquoise packet of gradations but knew from the beginning she wanted to expand it, colorwise.

At the fabric store where I work, and with the turquoise packet as a guide, Dorothy and I pulled a wide assortment of bolts of fabric that turned the monochromatic color scheme into an analogous color scheme. We avoided any values that were too dark or too light, but instead kept to the middle range.

Dorothy cut these fabrics into strips of equal width. However, when she pieced them together to create a fabric, she cut random lengths. Her background fabric is varied but subtle. Using her hand-dyed fabrics, she then cut and appliquéd leaves to the vest. The leaves are in contrast to the analogous background because they are monochromatic. This is a beautiful marriage of hand-dyed fabric with commercially dyed fabric. Dorothy's hand quilting design added to the movement of the leaves across the pieced field. Wearing the vest with a matching dress makes a very sophisticated, understated outfit.

Mary Russell has combined a printed fabric with a gradated pack and additional related solids to create "Token Tucks and Biscuits," shown in Color Plate 30. Mary, who enjoys working with simple design modules, created a square block made up of two rectangles and a square. She tucked some of her fabric and made several biscuit puffs. It was then fairly straightforward to compose the modules. At the top, Mary selected the lightest values of the gradation. As she worked her way down the asymmetrical front, she added darker values and dropped the lighter ones. When she reached the bottom rows, the floral print was added. It was repeated for the underlapping, minor front, and one of the underarm pieces.

Mary considered the design opportunities gradations provide when she trimmed the pieced front panel and covered her buttons. Attention to such details makes a decided difference in tying together the parts of a garment. Because Mary frequently sells her garments, she is particularly aware of her time investment. For this reason, she made a plain denim back. To add weight to counterbalance the pieced front, she added several vertical tucks to the back piece.

Pati Waterfield used a crane print as the starting point for her garment, "Birds of a Feather Flock." (See Color Plate 23.) She eliminated the lightest values from her gradated pack, but added black, red, and white chintz. Not only were some of the modules strip pieced, but the joining bias strips were also pieced. Slender Pati has created an animated, fun jacket that suits her personality.

Don't neglect glitz; it can add sparkle, focus, and fun to your hand-dyed fabrics. For example, Salle Crittenden used some slinky "evening" types of fabrics in "Oklahoma Crude." Students have also used lamé, both for puffs and as part of piecing designs. If you'd like to dress up your garment for formal occasions, this is certainly one way to go.

PUFFS

About the time I conceived of the pushed-neutral color scheme, I had gotten interested in tucking fabric. I liked the way this surface manipulation added a subtle textural interest to my garments and quilts without making a color change. So when I started exploring the uses of hand-dyed fabric, I decided to look for additional ways to manipulate fabric. An article in *Quilter's Newsletter Magazine* reminded me of the puff, or biscuit, Christmas wreaths we all made at the beginning of the quilting revival. In fact, I taught my high school quilting students to make them for years.

But how could they be adapted to clothing? The original squares had been stuffed with batting. This would never do; quilters were already concerned with looking too large in their quilted garments. What would happen if the stuffing step was just eliminated? I was onto something—low-cal puffs! Once the upper fabric was folded into position and stitched in place, it would never lie absolutely flat again. So it would add interest and texture, but not inches.

Making Puffs

Puffs are very simple to make. These directions make a finished 2½" puff (Figure 3-1):

1. Cut two squares of fabric:
   —One 4" x 4" square of your fashion fabric (what you will see on the outside when you're done)
   —One 3" x 3" square of backing fabric (muslin or some other plain fabric).
2. Mark the halfway point on the four edges of the backing fabric by folding the ends together and creasing them between your fingers.
3. Beginning on any side, pin the corners of the fashion fabric to the corners of the backing fabric. Place the pins perpendicular to the edge and close to the ends.

**Figure 3-1.
How to make
traditional puff
or biscuit.**

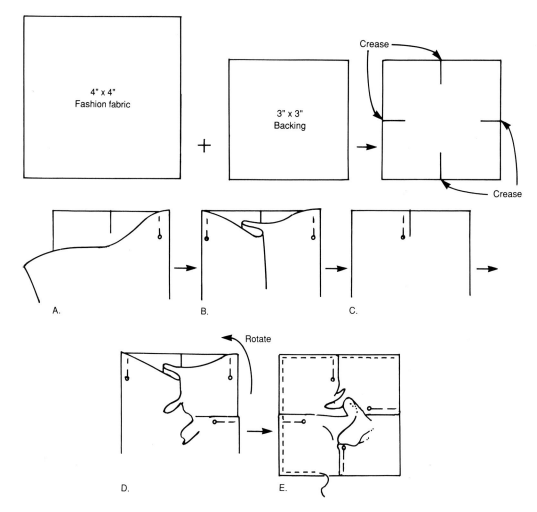

4. Flatten the fashion fabric by folding a pleat in it. Line up the top, outside, edge of the pleat with the halfway point crease mark. Pin in place with a perpendicular pin. (You will be sewing over this pin later, so make sure the head is away from the edge.) Remove the two end pins.
5. Continue in this manner by rotating your background fabric one turn, or 45°, and repeating Step 4 until all four sides have been pleated flat.
6. To hold the pleats in place until they're permanently stitched, machine-baste around the outside, ⅛" from the edge.

With these general directions, puff-making should be a breeze. Here are a few additional hints and tips to make the job even easier.

First of all, when calculating the size of the squares, always add in ½" to each side measurement to allow for the ¼" seam allowance all the way around. Cut the fashion fabric 1" larger than the backing fabric in both directions. This is in addition to the seam allowance. Since these are simple squares, the pieces can all be cut with a rotary cutter to save a little time.

I've found it works best to rotate the squares in the same direction as I fold in the fashion fabric on each of the four edges. It doesn't make any difference which direction, but consistency of method means a more consistent appearance.

And finally, when selecting a size, consider your own body size, flamboyance quotient, and the size of the area on the garment to be filled. As a guide, the puffs I used for "Route 66" are 2½" finished; Mary Russell used 2" finished puffs in her modules; Pati Waterfield used 3".

Shape and Origami Variations

Once you have mastered the folding of puffs, you will want to know what else you can do with them. Besides varying the size of your square, there are many more possibilities.

What about shape? Just because puffs have always been folded in squares is no reason they have to be confined to that shape. My students have tried rectangles and even triangles, and the answer is yes, they work, too.

**Photo 11. Where's the Orange? (detail).
Patricia Waterfield, Ridgefield, WA**

Pati Waterfield started with a triangle with a 3" base and height. Photo 11 shows a detail of her garment, "Where's the Orange?" Triangle puffs are alternated with plain triangles.

Figure 3-2 shows how to draw the two triangles for a triangle puff; use this information to experiment with other shapes. You may want to vary the amount of fabric added to the basic shape to create more fullness. For example, rather than just adding ½" extra, add ¾" and see if you like the results better. Once the fabrics are cut

and the halfway mark creased on the three sides, proceed with Steps 3 through 6 as described in making a traditional square puff.

When I teach my hand-dyed fabric class, I ask each student to fold a puff or biscuit for themselves so they will understand the process. And even though I try to give clear, concise directions, sometimes there's a glitch. Thank goodness Karyl Towse misheard my directions because in so doing, she invented the "origami" puff!

While completing Step 4 in the directions for a traditional square puff, she lined up the *underneath* rather than the top edge of the pleat with the halfway crease. When this is done to all four positions, a square *diamond* of fabric forms, rather than a puff. This can be caught with four little stitches from the wrong side to permanently hold the diamond in place. (See Figure 3-3.) When Carol Ann Wadley used origami puffs, she held her diamonds in place with gold studs. (See Photo 10.)

I used the origami puff when I made "Sunset: Coast Highway One." Color Plate 25 shows a detail of this alternate version. Notice it is much more classical or tailored in appearance. Those worried about adding excess bulk to the body will favor this version.

It's also possible to fold triangle puffs in this alternate way (Figure 3-4). In Photo 11 of Pati Waterfield's triangular puffs, the middle puff is on its way to forming a small origami triangle. Three stitches would hold the small triangle permanently in position.

**Figure 3-2.
Triangular puff.**

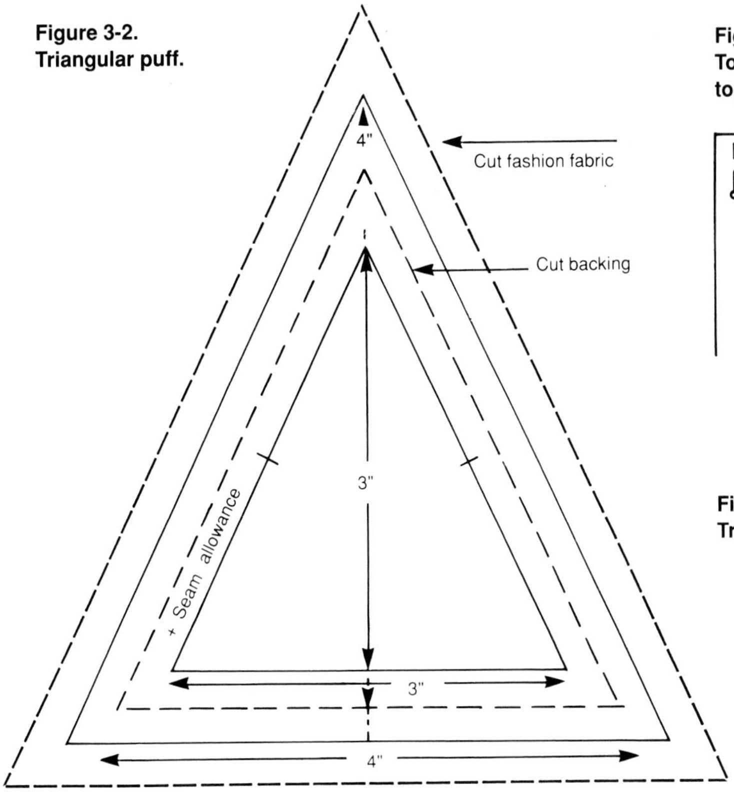

4"

Cut fashion fabric

Cut backing

+ Seam allowance

3"

3"

4"

**Figure 3-3.
To make origami puff, line up underneath fold rather than top fold.**

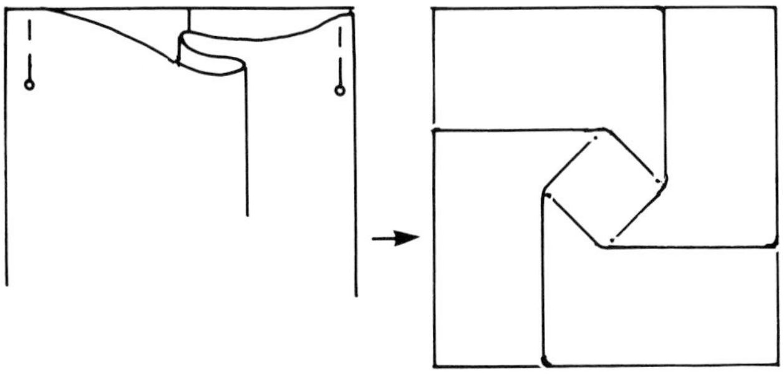

**Figure 3-4.
Triangular origami puff.**

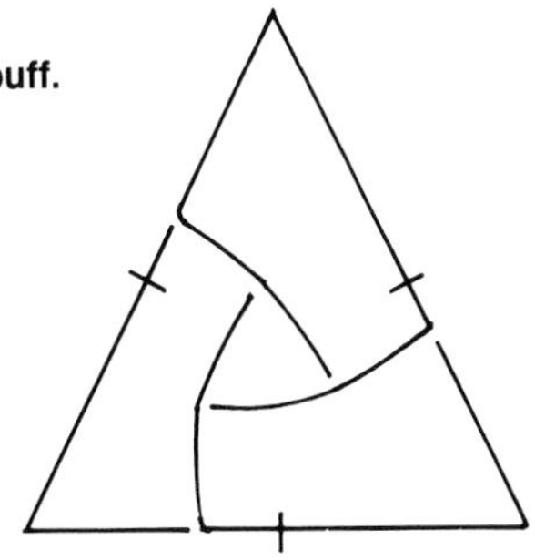

CREATING WITH MODULAR GRIDS

One of the easiest ways to begin using hand-dyed fabric is to devise some form of grid pattern to build your design around. The following suggestions should help you get started; you will undoubtedly be able to think of others once you get involved in using hand-dyed fabric in your garment plans.

Pieced Gradation Blocks + Gradation Puffs

I discovered the grid idea while making "Route 66." I had decided to set up an alternating pattern of biscuit puffs and pieced blocks; to begin I divided my pieced square into four equal triangles. Once an equal number of triangles were cut from each of my eight gradations, I started at position 1 (either the lightest or darkest end) and picked up four triangles, working my way down the color gradation. (See Photo 9.) For my first stack, I picked up triangles 1, 2, 3, and 4. Then I went on to position 2 and gathered triangles 2, 3, 4, and 5. Each time I picked up four triangles, I placed them in a little stack by themselves. I continued in this manner until all the triangles had been grouped.

When I began to arrange my first stack of triangles for piecing, I discovered the square didn't look right if I just put the triangles in sequential order because the lightest one touched the darkest one. I found the block more pleasing if the triangles were regrouped so the two lightest triangles were across from each other and the two darkest were across from each other. (See Figure 3-5.)

After all the triangles were pieced into squares, and the puffs were also made from the gradations, I randomly arranged them to cover my pattern pieces. Photo 12 shows some interesting secondary patterns that sometimes occurred when the puffs and triangles meet...an added bonus.

The same simple square shape can be divided in many ways. Figure 3-6 shows some additional possibilities.

Figure 3-5.
Arranging gradated triangles in a block.

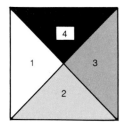 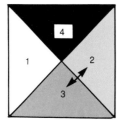

Rotate 2 & 3

Photo 12. Route 66 (detail). Mary Mashuta, Berkeley, CA

Figure 3-6.
Dividing a square into segments.

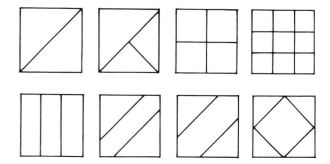

Stripped Gradation Blocks + Gradation Puffs

You could also stitch strips of even or random widths of your gradation and then randomly cut squares from these strips to mix with the puffs made from the gradations. It will be even more interesting if some of the squares are cut off-grain as Suzy Trandem did. She used lamé for a subtle accent. (See both Figure 3-7 and Photo 13.) Pati Waterfield also used some strip-pieced blocks in "Birds of a Feather Flock." (See Photo 18.)

Solid Gradation Blocks + Print

Commercially printed fabric, especially some of the wild designs available today, can be successfully combined with gradated hand-dyed fabric; color is the key in coordinating your fabrics. As an example, I cut out a set of squares from a gradation and placed them on a large, graphic print. I arranged my dyed fabric by gradation rather than placing it randomly. This is more subtle if you are trying to keep your garment understated. Mixing all the values randomly will create a spottier appearance if you prefer to make your garment more animated. (See Photos 14 and 15.)

**Figure 3-7.
Cutting strips into blocks.**

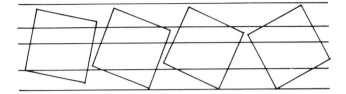

**Photo 13.
Works in progress
(detail). Susann
Trandem, San Luis
Obispo, CA**

that was made to go with my set of fabrics (which had been dyed from pink to blue). I rotary cut the alternating squares and randomly placed them. Note, however, that I organized my puffs by color to give order to the composition. (See Color Plates 24 and 25.)

**Photo 14.
Wild print + gradation.**

Solid Gradation Blocks + Print Puffs

When Carol Ann Wadley made "Western Roses," she combined part of a rose-colored gradation with a rose print which she had folded into her origami puffs (Photo 10). She used these on one front and part of the back of her vest. For the other front and the remaining back section, she used the right and wrong side of some denim fabric. The value reads the same for both the red and blue fronts, giving a balanced effect.

Print Blocks + Solid Gradation Puffs

You can switch and try combining your puffs made from a gradation with squares of a printed fabric. When I made "Sunset: Coast Highway One," I used handpainted fabric

**Photo 15.
Gradation squares +
wild print.**

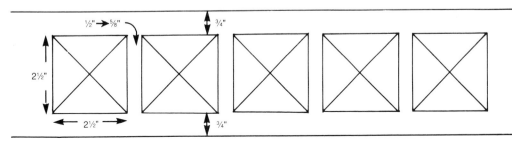

**Figure 3-8.
Hem detail. Janet
Paluch. Band
approximately 65"
long. (Work out
uneven fractions in
strips between the
squares.)**

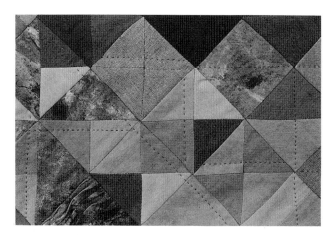

Photo 16. I Guess¿ That's Why They Call It the Blues (detail). Janet Paluch, Sacramento, CA

Pieced Blocks Alone

Anne Verhoeven used a grid of squares divided into triangles when she made "A Sleeve Short and Feeling Foolish," shown in Color Plates 16 and 17. Occasional unpieced squares are randomly added to the design. They are either puffs or stacked and slashed blocks.

In Color Plate 31, Janet Paluch's grid of 2" squares placed on point gives a fresh look to "I Guess¿ That's Why They Call It the Blues." Some of her squares are solid pieces; others are made of two, three, or four triangles. She freely mixed her gradation with jean fragments and commercial spatter-painted fabric. (See Photo 16.) Notice how her pieced design fits comfortably into the princess, or vertical, seaming of her Burda pattern. Also look at the shaped hem of the jacket. The diagonal zigzag lines keep the jacket from being boxy. Placing her squares on point also creates a slimming line.

To complete her outfit, Janet made a chambray denim skirt and trimmed the edge with alternating strips and squares as a subtle surprise. (See Figure 3-8.) The squares, made from slightly lighter chambray broadcloth which has been pieced into triangles, contrast subtly with the skirt fabric. In this way, not too much attention is called to the skirt; the trim is seen more as a backup area of design.

Pieced Modules

One other possibility is to create a pieced module which can be repeated over and over as Mary Russell did when creating "Token Tucks and Biscuits." (See Color Plate 30.) Her square was 3¼" x 3¼" and she began by placing a 2" square in one corner. Sometimes she placed puffs in this position, other times tucked fabric, her print, or a solid. (See Figure 3-9.)

(Chapter 3 continues after the Color Section.)

**Figure 3-9.
Mary Russell modules.**

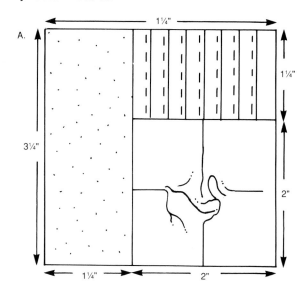

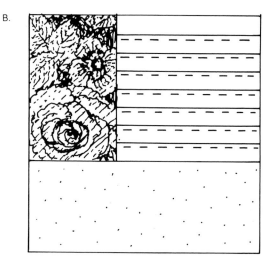

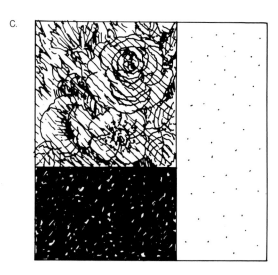

PUSHED NEUTRALS

3. Amtrak-Am-Slow.
   (detail)

1. Amtrak-Am-Slow.
   (worn with black)
   Mary Mashuta, Berkeley, CA

2. Amtrak-Am-Slow.
   (worn with gold and gray)

4. Eucalyptus.
Mary Mashuta,
Berkeley, CA

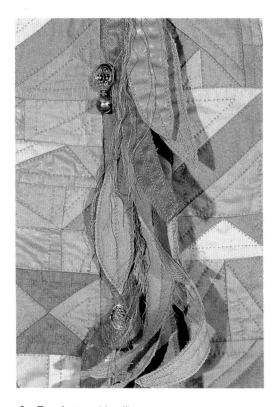

5. Eucalyptus. (detail)

6. Eucalyptus. (detail)

42

9. Softly Seminole. (front) Pam Quan, Orinda, CA

7. Desert Sky.
Rosalind Zinns,
Oakland, CA

8. Seaside. Dorothy Clarke, Walnut Creek, CA

10. Softly Seminole. (back)

11. Gray Study.
    Laura Munson Reinstatler,
    Mill Creek, WA

12. Gray Study.
    (detail)

13. Urban Lilacs. (left)
    (light-value blouse)
    Dorothy Clarke,
    Walnut Creek, CA

14. Urban Lilacs. (right)
    (medium-value blouse)

15. Moonbow Confetti.
Debra Millard Lunn,
Denver, CO

HAND-DYED FABRIC

16. A Sleeve Short and Feeling Foolish.
Anne Verhoeven, Portland, OR

17. A Sleeve Short and Feeling Foolish.
(detail)

18. **Midnight Rainbow.**
    Mary Mashuta,
    Berkeley, CA

19. **Daydreams.**
    (wrap right)
    Mary Mashuta,
    Berkeley, CA

20. **Daydreams.**
    (wrap left)

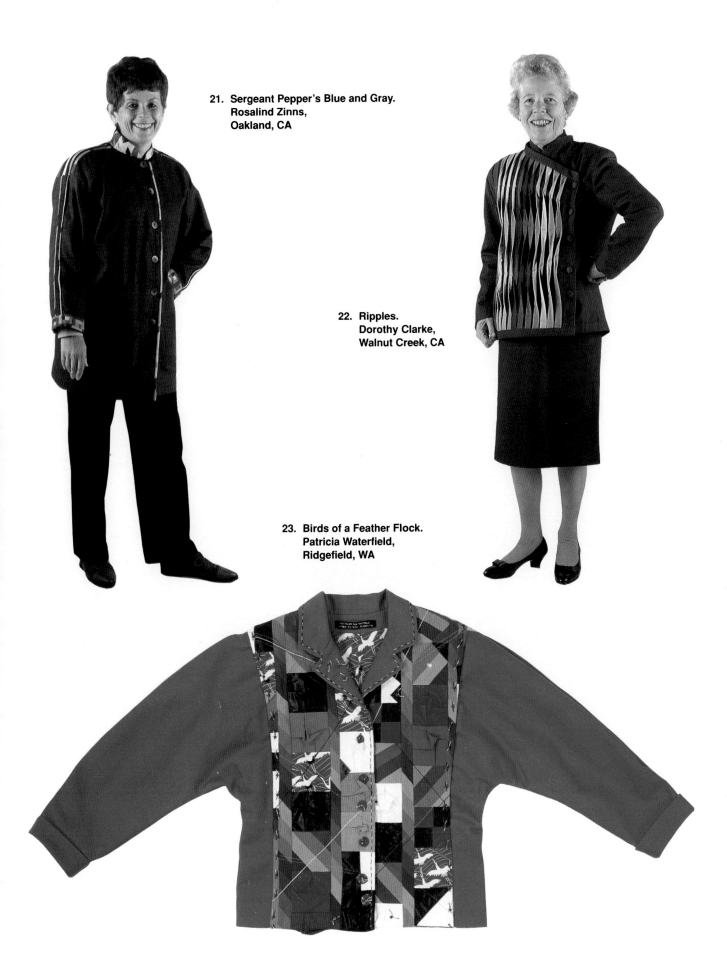

21. Sergeant Pepper's Blue and Gray.
Rosalind Zinns,
Oakland, CA

22. Ripples.
Dorothy Clarke,
Walnut Creek, CA

23. Birds of a Feather Flock.
Patricia Waterfield,
Ridgefield, WA

24. Sunset: Coast Highway One. Mary Mashuta, Berkeley, CA

25. Sunset: Coast Highway One. (detail)

26. Oklahoma Crude.
    Salle Crittenden,
    Alameda, CA

27. Oklahoma Crude.
    (detail)

28. Route 66.
    Mary Mashuta,
    Berkeley, CA

29. Route 66.
    (detail)

30. Token Tucks and Biscuits. Mary Russell, San Luis Obispo, CA

31. I Guess¿ That's Why They Call It the Blues.
Janet Paluch, Sacramento, CA

32. Leaves in a Gentle Breeze.
Dorothy Clarke,
Walnut Creek, CA

STRIPES

33. Raid at Julie's. Mary Russell, San Luis Obispo, CA

34. Dollars and Yen. Mary Russell, San Luis Obispo, CA

35. Tokyo Revisited. Anne Ito, Berkeley, CA

36. Tokyo Blues. Marion Ongerth, Berkeley, CA

37. A Stripe Is a Stripe, Is a Stripe. (front)
Mary Mashuta, Berkeley, CA

38. A Stripe Is a Stripe, Is a Stripe. (back)

39. Cover Stripes. Mary Mashuta, Berkeley, CA

41. Akasaka. (front detail)

42. Akasaka. (pant leg detail)

40. Akasaka. Mary Mashuta, Berkeley, CA

43. Almost Spools.
Deanna Charlton,
Shasta, CA

44. Red Knots.
Cathie Hoover,
Modesto, CA

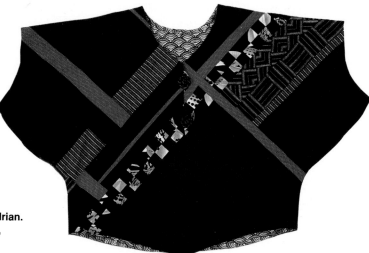

45. Japanese Mondrian.
Rosalind Zinns,
Oakland, CA

46. Autumn Stripes.
    (front)
    Elaine Anderson,
    Castro Valley, CA

47. Autumn Stripes.
(back)

48. Shooting Stars.
    Susan Smith,
    Danville, CA

49. Fascinating Lines.
Mabry Benson,
Kensington, CA

50. Fascinating Lines. (detail)

51. Stripe Medley.
Barbara Stinson,
Moraga, CA

52. Stripe Medley. (detail)

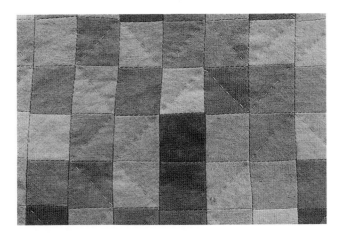

**Photo 17. Moonbow Confetti (detail).
Debra Millard Lunn, Denver, CO**

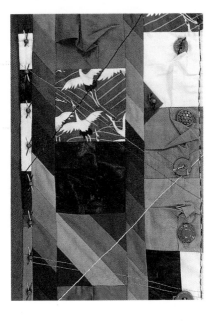

**Photo 18.
Birds of a Feather
Flock (detail).
Patricia Waterfield,
Ridgefield, WA**

TECHNICAL ADVICE FOR HAND-DYED FABRICS

Piecing accuracy is always important, but much of the piecing in the garments illustrated in this chapter was not as small-scale as it was in the preceding one. Therefore, it was easier to do. Let's look at some of the quilting used on the hand-dyed garments instead.

Hand and Machine Quilting

Hand quilting will show nicely on most hand-dyed fabrics if you want to do it. In "Route 66," I quilted the alternating pieced squares with turquoise thread. Quilting is placed close to the edge if there is no seam; ¼" away if there is a seam. Since the direction of pressing the seams was arbitrary, a random pattern which looks very contemporary was created. (See Photo 12.)

Janet Paluch has created a pleasing pattern of quilting over the pieced grid of squares she used in "I Guess¿ That's Why They Call It the Blues." (See Photo 16.) Each square is quilted in some way, but there is no set pattern as the random squares are made from one to four pieces. Remember, it isn't necessary to quilt each and every piece or segment.

Debra Millard Lunn also chose to hand quilt her "Moonbow Confetti" (Photo 17). She has created an interesting geometric pattern across her field of 1" squares. Again it isn't necessary to quilt every single square; in fact, this would be exceedingly tedious. Debra's pattern allows her to move diagonally across her squares from corner to corner as she stitches.

Since many of the hand-dyed garments use grids, it's possible to use machine quilting, following the techniques (especially stitching in the ditch and structural blind quilting) discussed in Chapter 6.

Pati Waterfield devised a creative alternative for machine quilting. (See Photo 18.) She randomly places straight lines of single or double machine stitching across the entire pieced surface. The thread color may match the fabric, or not. She also uses a machine zigzag stitch to couch, or hold in place and tack on, strands of perle cotton. By using one of the invisible nylon threads for her zigzag stitch, her "quilting" is hardly noticeable. You just see the perle cotton.

Quilting with Perle Cotton

Like many professional quilters, I seem to go from deadline to deadline. As soon as one project is completed and ticked off, another deadline appears on the horizon. This was the case when I was working on "Sunset: Coast Highway One." One day remained and I still had to do the quilting! There simply wasn't enough time to do the meticulous hand quilting I normally do. However, it was a shame to be so near to finishing and not make it. That was when I glanced up and saw the beautiful little balls of DMC perle cotton thread on the shelf in my studio. (This is one of the reasons I prefer open storage!)

I selected the two starting colors of my fabric, pink and blue. Perle cotton comes in a number of sizes, but I most often use size 5 which requires a large needle eye. I prefer fairly large Embroidery 1/5 needles. A yarn needle threader comes in handy.

Since I was using an alternating grid of puffs and solid squares, I decided to stitch only the plain squares. (See Color Plate 25.) Making the smallest stitches I could with the large needle, I stitched diagonally across the squares, one at a time. Pink stitches were worked in one direction; blue in the other. I wasn't sure how to hide the knots as my lining had already been inserted and the seams bound, so I just left them exposed and hanging. Each piece of thread has two double knots, one about an inch from the end, and the second about an inch away, right where the thread goes in or comes out of the fabric.

Whew, another deadline met! As I look at the garment now, I realize it's much more interesting because of this special quilting. Hand quilting would have been fine, but not nearly so exciting and animated.

EMBELLISHMENTS

While not always necessary, embellishments provide added interest when used on decorative garments. Let's look at some items selected by the makers of the garments who chose to use hand-dyed fabric. (Of course, these embellishments could be used with other types of fabric.)

Studs

Studs provide a satisfying way to add some sparkle to your creations. Sometimes, rhinestones and sequins are just too dressy and formal. While studs may seem inextricably connected with Western wear, with a little creative thought we can expand their design possibilities.

When I made "Route 66," I selected denim as the filler fabric. Color Plates 28 and 29 show the outfit and the wonderful 1950s silver-and-turquoise buttons I wanted to feature. Silver studs seemed a natural way to expand their importance. I embellished the front panels with alternating rows of round and square studs. The faceted square studs mirrored the piecing designs used in my alternating blocks; the round ones mirrored the round shape of the buttons.

Since I intended the flamboyance quotient to go fairly high on the outfit, I embellished the sleeves with smaller circle and triangle studs. The sleeves already were trimmed with zigzag denim strips; I didn't want to overwhelm and upstage them.

Next came the skirt. To highlight the detailing, I used straight rows of alternating round faceted and plain studs. This would call attention to the pockets, but not overly emphasize the hip area.

The studs moved from a supportive to commanding position on the skirt hem area. Diagonals and zigzags always catch the eye, so I arranged a pattern of alternating large and small round studs in a large zigzag pattern. The pattern of studs mirrored the denim strip trim on the sleeves and so my embellishments came full circle.

Carol Ann Wadley also chose studs for embellishment when she made "Western Roses." She used gold ones to tack the diamonds in her origami puffs in place. (See Photo 10.)

Buttons

Closures often play a less dramatic, but still important, part in the designing of a garment. For example, Mary Russell reinforced her progression from light to dark on the front of "Token Tucks and Biscuits" by covering buttons with fabric from her gradation. (See Color Plate 30.) Subtle details like this complement the overall design intention.

Salle Crittenden's favorite color scheme is black, white, and red. She wasn't happy with "Oklahoma Crude" until she was able to add a touch of red to enliven it. Large red triangle buttons mirror the zigzag of her trimming strips. To further tie in the red, and to spark up the more subtle pieced body of the jacket, she added an occasional red prairie point and a variety of small, triangular red buttons as embellishment (Color Plate 27).

Pati Waterfield approaches buttons from a fresh perspective. She has purposely chosen to use a set of mismatched red buttons as closures for her outfit, "Birds of a Feather Flock" (Photo 18). Pati has also freed herself from two other traditions concerning buttons. Even though I'm sure she was once taught how to sew on a button with sewing thread, she has let go of that information and found a more exciting way to accomplish this mundane task for her two-hole buttons. She has used perle cotton, and tied it in knots that show on the right side of the button rather than being hidden. The use of the heavier thread and knots complements her bead and embroidery embellishment.

Another tradition that Pati has gleefully disregarded is the "rule" that all buttonholes must be positioned either vertically or horizontally in the same garment. Not for Pati, whose small, but innovative, touches add whimsy and animation to her work.

Embroidery and Beads

I particularly enjoy quilts that give the viewer something to see close up as well as at a distance. It's much the same way with wearables. Fine quilting often does this, but other means of embellishment can also provide that important "take a closer look" charm. Embroidery and beads both add small, closeup detailing to garments.

Look again at Pati Waterfield's wonderful garment, "Birds of a Feather Flock" (Color Plate 23). As a finishing touch, she has added small red beads embroidered on with bold "X" stitches done in perle cotton. Details such as the thread embellishments offer yet another opportunity to repeat colors already used in the general color scheme. As an alternative to top stitching, Pati embroidered a threaded running stitch around the collar and down the jacket front. Little finishing details such as this make a surprising difference in the overall impact of the garment.

4
STRIPES

By definition, stripes are bands or streaks of a different color across a surface. To form a stripe pattern on fabric, it is necessary to have two different hues, or at least two different values of one hue. If the textile is woven, stripes can also be produced by changing the weaving pattern on a one-color fabric. This is called a self-colored stripe.

Beginning with these basic limitations, countless variations are possible. Stripes can be bold or demure, elegant or informal, outrageous or calm. Some are easier to work with than others, but all have the potential of creating optical effects which can be used to advantage in creating wearables.

What are some of the special qualities of stripes? Most important, because of their nature, they create directional pattern. Woven stripes are produced vertically or horizontally. The majority are vertical, running up and down, parallel to the selvage of the fabric. Dyed threads are used to produce woven stripes. This means that both sides of the fabric are the "right" side, a potential design bonus.

If the stripe is printed, there's only one "right" side, which can decidedly limit design choices. Printed stripes can also be either vertical or horizontal. In addition, they can be produced as a diagonal pattern since printed design is not dependent on the limitations of the loom.

CLASSIFICATION OF STRIPES

We know there are even and uneven plaids, but how does one classify stripes? There is no agreement, as yet, on the appropriate terms. We could easily, and accurately, use any of the following:

    even and uneven
    balanced and unbalanced
    reversible and nonreversible
    regular and irregular

However, I have decided to use "even" and "uneven" here because these terms make the most sense to me.

To decide which type of stripe you're looking at, pick a dominant line, if there is one, to act as a reference point. As other lines or stripes extend out to the left and right of your reference line, do they form mirror images of each other? If one line doesn't work, try using another. If you can discover a mirror image, you have an even stripe; if you can't find one, you have an uneven stripe. Look at some even stripes to get an idea of this (Photo 19).

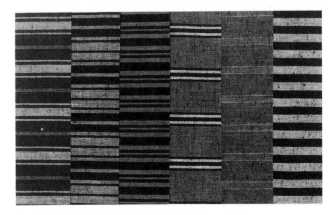

Photo 19. Even stripes.

Photo 20. Uneven stripes.

59

In uneven stripes, the pattern formed moves in only one direction. You can read the stripes in order from left to right from your reference line, but they don't, and can't, form a mirror image around it. A different stripe will be directly to the right of your reference line than is on its left. Look at some uneven stripes to see how they differ from even ones (Photo 20).

There are two other ways to check a stripe to see whether it is even or uneven in patterning. Fold the fabric back on itself so your fold line is parallel to the stripes.

Figure 4-1.

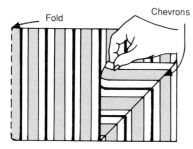

A. Woven even stripes chevron.

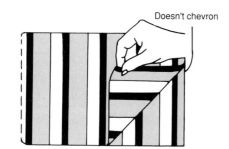

B. Woven uneven stripes don't chevron.

Figure 4-2.

A. Printed even stripes match when cut and rotated.

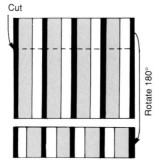

B. Printed uneven stripes don't match when cut and rotated.

(This is easier to see on a printed stripe if you fold the "good" side of the print to the inside.) Next, along the bottom edge, fold up a corner to form a triangle. Do these lines meet to form a chevron with the stripe underneath? If the lines chevron, you have an even stripe; if they don't chevron, you have an uneven stripe (Figure 4-1). An alternative method to folding fabric is to cut across your stripes with a cutting line perpendicular to the stripes. Rotate the cut piece 180° and see if you can match the pattern. If it matches, you have even stripes; if it doesn't, you have uneven stripes (Figure 4-2).

Stripe design repeats vary in width and may confuse the issue when you're trying to decide whether you have even or uneven stripes. The simplest repeat design would be made up of two lines in two different colors. Pin stripes would be an example. (Also see the first stripe in Photo 19.) In a repeat, the stripe width doesn't vary once established. If there is a size change, it means that the repeat is larger than you first thought. The size of a repeat may affect your design possibilities.

Japanese Stripes and Other Stripes

The striped fabrics used for the garments illustrated here are *tsumugi* and *tosan* fabrics woven in Japan. They are a little heavier than traditional patchwork fabrics, but are very easy to handle, cut, sew, and press. I have been fascinated with them for years. Unfortunately, I only decided to get serious about using them when it has become increasingly difficult to acquire them in the United States. They may not be available in your area unless you have a store that specializes in Japanese merchandise. Even then, stores may not have the fabric available because of current trade problems.

Mail-order purchase may be a good stripe solution. My line of "Shibui Stripes" plus some of the woven stripes in the "Lines" and "Mood Indigo" Collections by Roberta Horton, are suitable. I've seen Roberta's fabrics combined very successfully with Japanese fabrics. Check the Appendix under the Cotton Patch for address information.

Learn to go beyond "quilt" fabric. For example, try the decorator section in fabric stores. The fabric featured there is usually a heavier weight but could be quite usable, particularly with machine quilting. This fabric is also more expensive, but then again, it *is* wider.

Guatemalan fabric, with its heavier, looser weave, is another possibility. Make sure your pieces are cut on a larger scale since individual seams will be bulkier to handle with this type of fabric.

Striped fabrics provide an unexpected opportunity to cross (or at least mix and match) cultures by combining stripes from different countries. In my workshops, some wonderful juxtapositions have occurred when students bring stripes from their own collections and pair them with my Japanese stripes. For instance, look at the Mexican stripe paired with one of my Japanese stripes (Photo 21). Both fabrics were woven with orange, gold, green, beige, and black so they are comfortable with each other color-wise. The difference in scale between the two stripes makes for an exciting mix.

If you have a variety of stripes you would like to combine, but they don't quite go together colorwise, consider over-dyeing. One student had a collection of blue-and-white prints and stripes, all a little different from each other. By over-dyeing with Rit denim color, she was able to effectively combine them with some of my Japanese stripes. Anne Ito over-dyed her blue-and-white *yukata* lining in this way to tone the white part down so it would be more suitable when combined with the other, more elegant Japanese fabrics in her vest, "Tokyo Revisited." (See Color Plate 35.)

SELECTING COMPATIBLE FABRICS

I have an entire shelf of Japanese striped fabric rolls in my studio. When I begin to create, I tend to keep reaching for additional rolls as my design evolves. However, the amount of your striped fabric may be more limited. Remember your fabric can be "stretched" by combining it with solids and appropriate prints. When looking at fabrics available in quilt collections, some of the prints that feature abstract figures are appropriate; on the other hand, traditional calico just doesn't work (Photo 22).

Combining stripes with nontraditional quilt fabrics can produce exciting results. For example, Susan Smith teamed two very similar Japanese stripes with an abstract geometric decorator fabric when she created "Shooting Stars," shown in Color Plate 48. Things appear more complicated than they really are because her decorator fabric was enhanced by a subtle color change from darker to lighter values as the design progressed across the yardage. She was able to capitalize

**Photo 22.
Stripe pieced with
abstract print.**

on this effect when she cut out and arranged her pieces (Photo 23).

Roz Zinns combined a small amount of striped fabric with a nontraditional print and a number of solids in "Japanese Mondrian" (Color Plate 45). The print was a large-scale sea shell design, an unlikely choice to most people. However, Roz realized that when the fabric was cut into smaller, unrecognizable segments it would be very interesting designwise. The print provides a softening relief to the straight lines of the stripe, the grid quilting designs, and the diagonal set of the major design configurations.

Deanna Charlton enjoys working with scraps. I sent her a variety of small pieces of the Japanese stripes I love so much. Using this mixture, she was able to create her exciting garment, "Almost Spools." (See Color Plate 43.) She added solids when she pieced the basic design units. The stripes are set off by the addition of the solids which provides places for the eye to rest. She also introduced a subtle, large-scale plaid woven in India. It appears in a supportive function—as filler on one front, as part of the binding, and as the lining.

Mary Russell also did a good job of combining stripes with prints and solids in her piece, "Dollars and Yen." (See Color Plate 34.) The Japanese *yukata* prints are used to make summer kimonos. Mary was able to combine two types of Japanese ethnic fabrics quite successfully.

Photo 24 shows a close-up of the fabrics Kay Sakanashi purchased in Osaka, Japan, and combined with her stripes. Anne Ito also used an ethnic fabric from a trip to make "Tokyo Revisited" (Color Plate 35). Their use of fabric from their travels, fabric filled with memories, reminds me how important it can be to move past the "preciousness" of some of the fabrics in our collections. If we never get around to using those oh-so-meaningful textiles, others won't have the pleasure of the personal associations that link us to our special fabrics. Why not use them and recall these memories as we sew and as we wear the finished garment? Why not share those memories with others, rather than leaving them on our fabric shelves?

Photo 21. Mexican stripe with Japanese stripe.

Photo 23. Shooting Stars (detail). Susan Smith, Danville, CA

Photo 24. Osaka (detail). Kay Sakanashi, Richmond, CA

Cathie Hoover loves scrap quilts and wanted to create that same exuberance in a wearable (Photo 25). She used many fabrics to create a scrap feeling in the interwoven design of "Red Knots," including Japanese *yukatas* and *ikats*, Dutch wax batiks, homespun plaid, a selection of quilt prints, plus several Japanese stripes. To establish some sort of order to the varied patterns, Cathie limited herself to a palette of blue, red, and golden beige.

One caution, especially if you are a beginner: if you combine stripes with other fabrics, make sure the two fabrics are integrated in your composition. This is the commonest error I see in classes. Students piece some motifs using their stripes and then piece some other motifs using their solids. Then they expect the two to magically go together, even though it's much like mixing oil and water. The easiest way to mix two kinds of fabric is to include them both in the same pieced block. (See Photo 22.) If you're creating an all-over fabric, the simple continued repetiton of the two kinds of fabric will accomplish this.

Beginning with Stripes

When you've decided to combine several stripes, where do you start when assembling possible fabrics? For beginners, especially, it's important to make sure the stripes are related in some way; more advanced sewers can be more adventuresome. For example, I usually start with several stripes that are somehow related to each other by color and fabric type. In my case, they would most likely all be Japanese stripes. The palette created may encompass a number of different colors, but some or all of the colors repeat from piece to piece. At least intuitively, there's an overall harmonious feeling that pleases me.

The feeling of harmony may vary from person to person as we all have different flamboyance quotients. Think about your "clutter tolerance," how much design,

Photo 25. Red Knots (detail). Cathie Hoover, Modesto, CA

pattern, and embellishment you like to see at once. A collection of fabrics that looks exciting to an understated person may seem boring to an extrovert. On the other hand, an extrovert's choices might overwhelm the understated person. Trust your intuition for what feels right for you.

Color Schemes

The colors used to form stripe patterns are the starting points for building a color scheme. When combining several stripes and/or adding prints and solids, expanding the beginning scheme becomes possible.

Monochromatic garments are more understated than garments with many colors vying for attention. Mary Russell's "Raid at Julie's" and "Dollars and Yen" are good examples of monochromatic color schemes. (See

Color Plates 33 and 34.) There is variety in the blues selected, but all are blue. This variety makes it easy for Mary's garments to be worn with any pair of jeans in her closet. By choosing to use both warm and cool blues, she has also overcome the quilter's tendency to overmatch. Her garments have life and are more exciting visually because the fabrics don't match perfectly.

If your choice of striped fabrics seems too ho-hum to you, try introducing a "foreigner" stripe, solid, or print that is considerably different in color. As an accent, it will spark colors in the other fabrics. If you are undecided about where to start in picking a color, try a complement of your main color. For example, Marion Ongerth introduced an orange stripe in "Tokyo Blues" (Color Plate 36). Orange, the complement of blue, her main color, is used on the front, near the face. The viewer's eye is drawn upward to the face of the wearer by this clever, foreigner color.

A word of caution: it's best to repeat the accent color once it's introduced or the eye of the viewer will go to the accent like a bullseye and be unable to keep moving. I call this the "stranger in paradise" phenomenom. Find at least one or two other places to repeat the color in the composition of the whole garment. Then the eye will move again and take in the entire creation.

The stripes that Elaine Anderson chose to work with presented a palate of golds and olive greens. (See Color Plates 46 and 47.) To carry out the color theme of "Autumn Stripes" established by her stripes, she assembled a selection of abstract prints and solids. To her surprise, she found more than she could possibly use in one garment so one of her tasks was to pare down the possibilities. She decided to use a lovely Japanese print on the outside bands and a more inexpensive domestic print for the lining.

My "Akasaka" was constructed from four stripes. (See Color Plates 40 through 42.) Black or red were each found in three of the four; the accent colors of gold or yellow appeared in two. The repetition of the colors from fabric to fabric established the basic color scheme and tied the fabrics together even though not every color appeared in every fabric. Since I was not mixing the stripes with solids or prints in my piecing, it became important that each stripe should be able to stand on its own when combined with the other stripes so the pattern would read clearly. Having color variation between the individual stripe patterns helped accomplish this.

The fabric featured in the photos on the front and back covers and in Color Plate 39 is an advanced design. "Cover Stripes" has color variety—not all the stripes have the exact same colors—but there is a color feeling that runs through the entire collection. Even though colors repeat from stripe to stripe, a particular color is not necessarily found in all seven stripe patterns.

When you have assembled the stripes and fabrics that make up your color scheme, check the value contrast of the colors. Remember that less contrast equals more understatment; higher contrast produces a more showy garment.

Variety and Limitations

When a garment is finished, what makes the parts go together? Similar colors and similar fabrics help tie the parts together. But for a wearable art garment to hold our attention, it needs sufficient variety as well as sufficient similarity.

When working with more than one stripe, I find the garment may be more interesting if there's some variety in the scale of the stripes used. For example, in "Akasaka" I used two small-scale stripes, one medium stripe, and one large, bolder stripe. (See Photo 28.)

Keep in mind your flamboyance quotient as you decide how much you want to have happening in your garment. Match the garment to you. Rely on your intuition; it will let you know if you've gotten carried away.

Because there may be limited amounts of some of your fabric selections available, keep those pieces particularly in mind as you create. For example, when I began piecing "Cover Stripes," I had only small scraps of my two favorite stripes (Color Plate 39). They had been purchased years before at a Kasuri Dyeworks scrap sale and were a treasured part of my fabric collection. In the end, the dimensions of the smallest determined the size of one of my pattern pieces. With careful cutting, I was able to cut six of it, eight of the other.

When these pieces were cut, that was all there was and I had to get creative. Rather than scattering them, I maximized their effect by clustering them on one of the front pieces. One piece escapes to the second front as a way of tying the two sides together; none is seen on the back.

Often I'm unsure how fabric will ultimately be used when I add it to my collection. Since space and funds are always a factor, I've learned to buy arbitrary amounts of fabric, generally a half-yard. I prefer to own four different half-yard pieces rather than two yards of the same thing. Later I may be sorry, but in the long run, I usually do my most creative work when I'm about to run out of my "favorite" fabric. Especially when buying stripes, you might want to be more generous than I am in the size of pieces purchased. The design limitations stripes impose, by their very nature, often mean a considerable amount of fabric waste as you pursue a particular design—your fabric may run out sooner than expected.

DESIGNING WITH STRIPES

To begin with, I don't worry about what will go where. I just try to come up with a pleasing unit, or units, which can become the basic building blocks to fill my garment pieces. It's possible to pick one unit and base the design of the entire garment on that unit—in essence, to manufacture one's own fabric. "Akasaka" is an example of this approach. (See Color Plates 40 through 42.) A 2½" square is used throughout. (Corresponding triangles completed the design in some areas.)

Sometimes I use a variety of modules or blocks. "A Stripe Is a Stripe, Is a Stripe" is an example of this method. (See Color Plates 37 and 38.) I created a variety of units and then figured out a way to tie them all together. Read on and see which approach appeals to you.

Stripes offer a new world of optical design possibilities, but you have to learn to *think stripes.* You may devise designs that surprise even you once you allow yourself the luxury of playing a little.

Because of the directional pattern in the fabric design, optical illusions can be created as the stripe pattern meets itself. Simple pattern shapes are all that is necessary to begin designing. Individual pieces can be fairly large, but keep in mind the scale of the pattern pieces in relation to the garment size, the size of the stripes being used, and your body size. You also need to be aware of the size of the optical units created. Since the lines can merge to form larger patterns, the actual cut size of the individual pieces may be obscured, and their total design effect may become much larger than anticipated.

Beginning

A good way to start playing is to take several pieces of white paper and cut geometric-shaped windows in them (Figure 4-3). Begin by cutting squares of varying sizes. Try a 2½" square and a 3" square. You may also want to draw the squares on point. On another piece of paper, try three triangles: 2", 2¼", and 2½". Then try rectangles, diamonds, and a 1" x 6" window to represent bias. When you move these windows back and forth over your fabric (up, down, crosswise, diagonally) you'll see only limited portions of the fabric, giving you an idea of how each shape will look when cut out.

This simple exercise shows there may be quite a difference in how the stripe appears when featured in the various windows. It can also help you decide which is a good size unit to use.

Designing with Squares

The square is the simplest shape to cut and sew. Stripes can be lined up parallel to the edge of the square or run diagonally, point to point, from corner to corner. You can cut identical repetitive units using a plastic template. Placing registration marks on your template ensures accuracy of placement, and makes it possible to create wonderful optical illusions (Figure 4-4).

Figure 4-3.
Geometric shapes for windows.

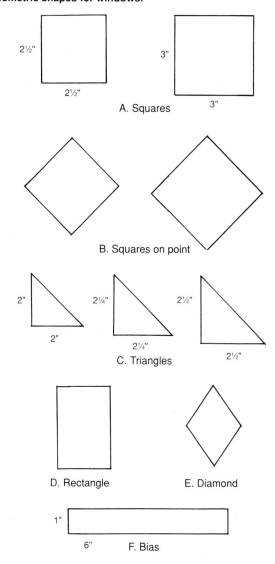

A. Squares

B. Squares on point

C. Triangles

D. Rectangle   E. Diamond

F. Bias

Two simple vests by Pam Quan and Kay Sakanashi are good examples of first projects using striped fabric cut into squares. Pam used three stripes: two were even, one was uneven, all were cut randomly. She lined up the stripes with a ruler edge, then cut strips with her rotary cutter. These were then cut into squares. She didn't worry about where the individual lines fell; she just cut (Photo 26). Pam decided to run the majority of her stripes vertically when composing her design. If she had consistently alternated verticals and horizontals, she'd have created a woven appearance.

Pam's patchwork makes up the major front and roughly two-thirds of the back of her vest. The leftover area, the minor front and the remaining back, is filled-in with one of the stripes placed on-grain vertically. The overlapping, shaped front, and staggered back placement of the squares, makes for a clean, simple, neat

Figure 4-4.
Registration marks on template ensure accuracy.

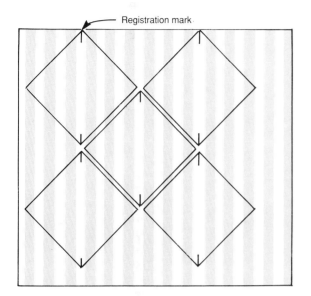

In a more complicated project, I used a finished 2½" square as my design shape for "Akasaka" (Photos 28 and 29). I first cut a set of 12 identical squares from a black-and-white stripe. The squares were drawn on point and featured the same white line placed diagonally from corner to corner. It was easy to lay the squares on other stripes to see what kinds of optical effects would occur. I used four even stripes of varying scale for the outfit. Only three stripes were used in the squares. One stripe was saved, cut on the bias, and then used for accent strips and cording.

For the right front, I used stripes A and B; for the left front, stripes B and C; and for the back, stripe C with a band of A and B.

By the time I got to the pants, I was short on fabric. Because I didn't have enough to make the pants from just one stripe, I got creative and made each leg a different color stripe. I purposely used the two more understated stripes from the original set. Two pieced strips, made of squares made from the stripes used for the other leg, were added. These were easy to set in because I had selected a pattern without a side seam.

If your time commitment is limited or if your flamboyance quotient is lower than mine, a less dramatic effect could be achieved by making the pants from just one stripe and/or by eliminating the wide strips running down the legs. As a more understated accent, or if you are particularly self-conscious about your hips, a thin, unbold strip would add a slimming line, leading the eye up and down. A bias cut would be the most desirable because it wouldn't be such an abrupt direction change.

As an example of a more complicated design using a square, Barbara Stinson took the simple shape as the

Photo 26. Samurai Stripes. Pam Quan, Orinda, CA

design which is easy to wear. To dress up her garment, Pam added a bias binding and a looped toggle closure.

In a comparable vest (Photo 27), Kay combined two similar, even stripes, cut diagonally on point with a template, with a special set of handprinted indigo fabrics from Osaka, Japan. The overlapping major front and the back are pieced in this simple repetitive design. Again, one front is left unpieced as a foil to showcase the design area on the major front. Kay highlighted her irregular edge with a plain cording for a neat finish.

Photo 27. Osaka. Kay Sakanashi, Richmond, CA

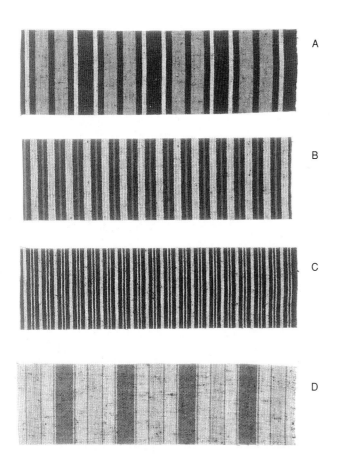

Photo 28. Akasaka fabrics.

Photo 29. Akasaka (top & pants). Mary Mashuta, Berkeley, CA

basic building block of her wonderfully optical creation, "Stripe Medley," shown in Color Plates 51 and 52. Her 2" finished pieces were cut from three even, differently scaled stripes placed on point. Clustering the squares in groups of threes, she was able to create an interlocking design.

Designing with Triangles

Now try your triangular shaped windows. Place one on the fabric so the stripe forms a right angle with the hypotenuse, or diagonal, of the triangle. If you have an even stripe, it's easy to find a pleasing mirror image. By cutting four matching triangles from your fabric and arranging them to form a larger square, you create an optical chevron. If you select a large, bold stripe to feature in the center of each triangle as I did in the detail of "Cover Stripes," a bold pattern with an "X" effect results; smaller, more even stripes create a subtler chevron pattern (Photo 30).

If you're working with an uneven stripe, though, you can't create an optical "X" by using this method. However, by carefully cutting a matched set of triangles in which you place the same set of lines parallel to the hypotenuse, you can still create a chevron when the

points of the four triangles meet. The optical effect is a series of squares as shown in Photo 31.

Anne Ito used an uneven stripe, with a large repeat, cut in this way to create the wonderful optical design in "Tokyo Revisited" (Photo 32). To further complicate the design, she used sets of triangles cut at different places on the unevenly placed lines. When she formed her squares from the triangles, she always selected three triangles that matched and finished the square with one that didn't. This was also a device for stretching the available fabric.

Roz Zinns used two even black-and-white stripes in "Japanese Mondrian" (Photo 33). Using squares and triangles from one of the stripes, she placed the base of her triangle along the stripe so that the other side forming the angle would be perpendicular to the base line. Four triangles were joined to form squares, but the chevron patterns were created by triangles in adjoining squares meeting, resulting in a wonderful interwoven effect.

In the three garments, "Cover Stripes," "Tokyo Revisited," and "Japanese Mondrian," the stripe has been placed perpendicular to the diagonal, perpendicular to the base, and parallel to the diagonal—three different possibilities for using a triangle shape with striped fabric.

Photo 30. Cover Stripes ("X" effect).
Mary Mashuta, Berkeley, CA

Photo 32. Tokyo Revisited (detail).
Anne Ito, Berkeley, CA

Photo 31. Cover Stripes ("Square" effect).
Mary Mashuta, Berkeley, CA

Photo 33. Japanese Mondrian (detail).
Rosalind Zinns, Oakland, CA

Susan Smith created a design using both squares and triangles for "Shooting Stars." The all-over repeat design was accomplished by combining squares with triangles pieced with a decorator print. Asking "what would happen if" let her discover she could produce a pattern which consisted of repeated twirling stars and squares on point. (See Photo 23.)

Other Repetitive Design Shapes

Any shape can be the starting point for a repetitive design. Doodling is a particularly helpful way to create these shapes. Draw a series of squares and then divide each one using as few lines as possible (Figure 4-5). A square divided in half, as in Block A, is obvious but how else could it be divided diagonally?

Once you have found a unit that pleases you, audition suitable fabrics to use in the segments by using the window idea (Figure 4-6). For example, I selected Block E. Since it was divided into three smaller segments, I redrew it three times. In each of the three new squares, I cut out a different portion to use as a window. Now

fabrics can be placed in each of the windows to get an idea of what should go where and what the finished block would look like.

Mary Russell used Block B which she drew as a 4" square. The block is divided by an off-center diagonal line. As she drew the line, she shifted it one inch from the corners. The resulting division of the square produced two identical but irregular geometric shapes. This simple design device made her basic block look far more interesting than if she had merely divided it into two equal triangles.

Mary made two garments using Block B. For her piece "Raid at Julie's," she limited her selection of fabrics to stripes as she created her modules. She increased the possible combinations by cutting each of the three stripes both horizontally and vertically (Photo 34).

For "Dollars and Yen," Mary added prints to the left-over stripes. She even cut stripe pieces off-grain because she was running out of fabric (Photo 35). As in antique quilts, cutting off-grain adds animation and life to the composition even though it's very difficult for most quilters to do it.

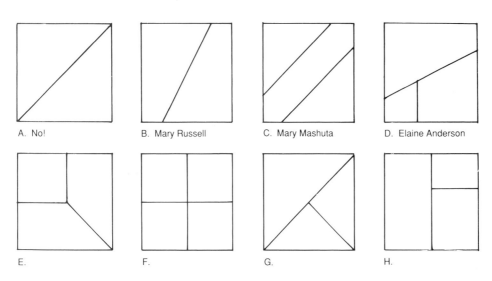

**Figure 4-5.
Square doodles.**

A. No!   B. Mary Russell   C. Mary Mashuta   D. Elaine Anderson

E.   F.   G.   H.

**Figure 4-6.
Making windows to
audition fabric.**

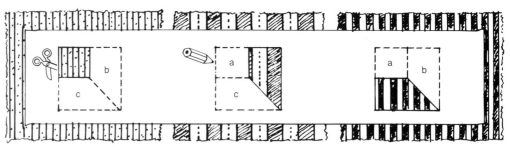

**Photo 34. Raid at Julie's (detail).
Mary Russell, San Luis Obispo, CA**

**Photo 35. Dollars and Yen (detail). Mary Russell,
San Luis Obispo, CA**

Elaine Anderson chose a similar basic square, Block D, but she added one more design line. Her repeated block is pieced from two stripes and one print (Photo 36). The design unit is repeated in two straight lines on the front and two diagonal lines on the back of "Autumn Stripes" (Color Plates 46 and 47). In Elaine's garment, where the leftover areas were filled with strip piecing and simple squares, so much was already happening that the garment needed to be calmed down by repeating identical units.

However, to add complexity to the overall design, Elaine used a checkerboard grid twice, once pieced in solids, another time pieced in stripes. The use of the stripes in the checkerboard configuration creates a feeling of weaving. Repetition of basic units in a garment helps tie the individual parts together even if they aren't colored in the same way.

Repetition of prints in different areas of the garment accomplishes the same goal. Elaine used a handsome Japanese abstract line print as the smallest segment of her square modules and for the collar and arm bands. Cording set off and highlighted these banded areas. The larger gold cording, used on the neck area only, helps to focus attention on the wearer's face.

Even though my "Cover Stripes" has some fairly complicated optical effects, a simple module was the basis of the design. I began with Block C and drew it as a 3½" square divided with a 1⅜"-wide diagonal strip. As they were assembled, the squares created larger optical modules. (See Color Plate 39.) Careful sewing was a must for the design to work. A pin-up wall can assist greatly when creating a piece like this, where it's necessary for the design to flow from pattern piece to pattern piece as it changes.

This design was particularly complicated because I had to keep in mind two separate parts of the design as it evolved. One design was formed as each set of four triangles met. Another was created from the diagonal bars interacting as they met and formed a diagonal pattern. Small secondary patterns also formed as four diagonal bars met and formed an "X." Many things to keep in mind at once....

For "Almost Spools," Deanna Charlton designed a basic block and then generated variations of it which could be contained in the original size square (Photo 37). She varied the width of the side pieces, thus changing the size and placement of the center rectangle. This fit in well with her desire to create a scrap look with the fabrics in her vest. After the individual blocks were pieced and joined, the resulting strips were placed on a gentle, or "soft," diagonal across the garment pieces. This added sophistication to the composition. (See Color Plate 43.)

Bias

The special effect that bias can contribute to your design cannot be underestimated. So much from so little! Used in individual strips it can act as a good divider of design areas. Mary Russell's work is a good example of this. In both "Raid at Julie's" and "Dollars and Yen," Mary set off the major design areas with striped bias strips of varying widths. (See Color Plates 33 and 34.) Usually bias is cut on a 45° angle, but for one strip Mary used a 60° angle instead. This is always an option when you don't have enough fabric to cut a smaller angle.

If you think you'll want some bias strips, and your fabric is limited, cut the strips first to ensure there'll be adequate fabric available. Sometimes you can get caught short if you leave this step to last.

Marion Ongerth created an understated repeat design from stripes cut as bias strips for "Tokyo Blues" (Photo 38). From a basic pattern established from sewing pieces cut 1½" x 1½" to 1½" x 3½", she created an all-over optical pattern. The design consistently repeated, but different stripes were inserted into the pattern as it moved along.

Photo 36. **Autumn Stripes** (detail).
Elaine Anderson, Castro Valley, CA

Photo 37. **Almost Spools** (detail).
Deanna Charlton, Shasta, CA

Photo 38. **Tokyo Blues** (detail).
Marion Ongerth, Berkeley, CA

Cathie Hoover used bias strips, turning some over to the other side so they would chevron, for some of the optical weaving strips in her vest "Red Knots." (See Photo 25.) The directional lines created by the chevrons help move the eye through a surface created from many varied patterns.

Striped bias trim is a nice finishing accent, too, becoming an opportunity for a last statement. Since it adds more pattern to the all-over design picture, keep in mind your flamboyance quotient and how much is already going on in the piece. Cathie Hoover trimmed her piece with bias and so did Pam Quan. However, Pam's vest was much more understated. Compare Cathie's vest (Color Plate 44) and Pam's (Photo 26).

Remember, too, that bias trim can usually be turned to the inside if you feel it adds too much activity to your design. Then you would only glimpse it by chance or when the garment was on display. Even though all the edges of "A Stripe is a Stripe, Is a Stripe" are finished with bias trim, only the lower edge shows when the garment is worn. (See Color Plates 37 and 38.)

Filler

It isn't necessary to have the entire design surface pieced. Solid and print areas can be introduced as filler and to give variety. Solids, particularly, can provide resting points for the eyes. Solid areas can also furnish a place for quilting and surface embellishment.

Plain, unpieced stripes can be used as filler, too. They are a good choice for minor fronts in asymmetrical garments. Pam Quan, Kay Sakanashi, and Susan Smith all used such minor fronts. In "A Stripe Is a Stripe, Is a Stripe," I used three unevenly cut bias strips pieced together to make fabric to be used as a filler on the back piece. (See Color Plate 38.)

Other Directions

"The sky's the limit" as far as stripes are concerned. Start simple: learn to look for stripe patterns in your environment, learn to let go and play with your fabric, and learn to ask, "what would happen if...?" Mabry Benson's coat, "Fascinating Lines," is an example of pulling out all the stops as far as stripes are concerned. (See Color Plates 49 and 50.) Using only one uneven stripe with a large repeat, she created varying sized pieced squares and rectangles; she also employed bias strips. Somehow she has put it all together to produce her own pieced fabric for front, back, and sleeves. And, to top it all, the garment is understated and easy to wear because she limited herself to a two-color maroon and indigo stripe with low value contrast. The two hues are discernably different, but the color change is not abrupt in feeling. The eye flows over the whole garment before it settles down to take in individual parts and wonder how in the world did Mabry do it?

TECHNICAL ADVICE FOR STRIPES

When you're ready to cut your fabric, remember to add seam allowances when you draw your templates. If you have been looking through windows it is all too easy to forget this. Plastic template material will let you see where the seams will fall when placing the template on the fabric. Registration marks, such as those used in stenciling, drawn on the template itself will help you cut like pieces the same.

When you cut out your pieces, the larger fabric may begin to look like Swiss cheese because you will be using only part of the actual design. How wasteful your cutting is depends on the scale of the pattern, the size of the repeat, and the size of the template you are tracing. Allow yourself ample extra yardage to begin with, learn to experiment with leftovers, and be creative (Figure 4-7).

Even stripes offer more possibilities when you are trying to create optical effects, but both even and uneven stripes can be used to advantage. Just keep straight which kind you're working with as the templates are placed on the fabric and the pieces are assembled for sewing. Remember, if you are working with uneven, woven stripes, the "wrong" side can be used to provide a reverse image.

If you are just beginning to understand stripes and still find yourself easily confused, schedule a quiet time for your cutting. If it's any consolation, confusion often occurs right before a learning breakthrough. Just hang in there and be patient!

Assembly and Sewing

A pin-up wall helps keep the individual pieces organized. If you don't have one, try to clear an area on your worktable large enough to spread out the pieces. Sometimes, the floor is the only space available, but it's harder to stand back and get perspective on your design.

When working with optical designs, it's especially important to be able to see the big picture. It's all too easy to inadvertently turn a single piece the wrong direction. As I sew, I keep checking my work against the design laid out before me. It is much better to discover a

Figure 4-7.
Planning ahead pays off.

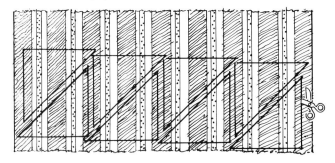

mistake early in the process than to have to rip it out after it has been surrounded by many carefully wrought seams.

Blocks can be sewn individually, but because most of us work with time restrictions, streamlined sewing procedures are important. It's particularly time effective to sew a number of seams at once, a process referred to as "tandem piecing" or "railroading." Organize complicated piecing more efficiently by analyzing the individual steps involved and devising a system for assembling a number of similar blocks at the same time.

As an example, here's the procedure I used for assembling the optical blocks used in piecing the fairly complicated design for "Cover Stripes," but the procedure could be applied to much simpler designs. (Actually, there were only two pattern templates used. Pieces 2 and 3 are identical, but to reduce confusion, I have given them different numbers.)

1. Lay out the entire design if it is an overall optical design with subtle changes from block to block. In simpler, repetitive designs, lay out at least an entire row of blocks (Figure 4-8).
2. Starting at the left edge (right edge for lefties), pick up Pieces 1 and 2, matching them together as they will be sewn. Pick up the pieces in order across the whole row. *(Hint:* If you aren't pinning them as you go, make sure you stagger each pair as you place them on the pile.)
3. Sew the whole row of seams; cut all threads; press all seams in the same direction.
4. Lay the stitched segments back down in order, making sure your optical design is maintained. If you have been careful, they should always be in order, though the order may be reversed. Mine are usually stacked in order from right to left, so I find it helpful to mark the first segment with a pin.
5. Pick up Pieces 1 and 3 and sew them together. Then press.
6. Lay this stitched segment back in place. Check to see all your patterns are being maintained. With both major and minor optical patterns developing, I did some especially careful checking.
7. If your block has more pieces, continue until all the segments have been joined to form the individual blocks.

Once you have assembled your individual blocks, read the sections on assembly and quilting in Chapter 6.

Hand and Machine Quilting

The pattern produced by stripes makes hand quilting difficult to see. For this reason, only two of the garments in this book were hand quilted. In "A Stripe Is a Stripe, Is a

Figure 4-8.
Order of sewing and assembly of "Cover Stripes."

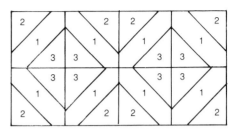

A. Lay out optical design.

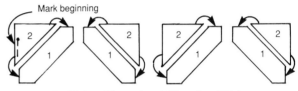

B. Pick up Pieces 1 and 2 in order. Stitch.

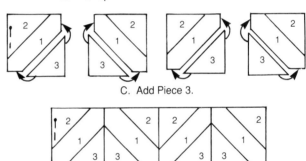

C. Add Piece 3.

D. Always lay back down in order to check.

Stripe," hand quilting was confined to the solid fabric included in the piecing. (See Color Plates 37 and 38.) However, there's a lot of quilting done by machine in the piece, most noticeably the double lines of stitching around the zipper. In other areas, the stitching, done in matching thread, is hidden in the woven pattern. Even I —who did it!—have to look closely to see the stitching. Its main function is structural; it holds the pieced top to the flannel batting. The stitching was not done through the lining which was inserted separately after the quilting was finished and the individual pieces trued-up.

For the other example of hand quilting shown in this book, see Deanna Charlton's lovely work in "Almost Spools" (Photo 37). The stitching shows up on the stripes because it meanders in soft loops across the straight lines. She confines the quilting to the center sections of her pieced blocks which are made from the stripes or solid red, and to the adjacent minor areas, made from solid black and a large-scale plaid fabric.

My advice about using hand quilting on stripes? Use it only if it shows. Don't waste hours of your valuable time doing something that not even you can see!

Photo 39. Red Knots (detail). Cathie Hoover, Modesto, CA

Look at the quilting for "Sunset: Coast Highway One" in Color Plate 25. This effect can be adapted for stripes. Light-colored, demure, understated stripes can be quilted diagonally with a stronger color, with the large areas formed by the stripes in bolder patterns quilted in contrasting colors. For ideas about quilting in plain areas, see the following section on sashiko embroidery.

You may prefer using machine quilting when you are working with stripes. Match your thread color to the predominant stripe color or select a neutral shade. Since your stripes may be multicolored, this could be the perfect time to try the nylon thread popular in the machine quilting of quilts. It comes in both clear and a medium shade for darker work. Use a neutral cotton thread in the bobbin.

Marion Ongerth used machine quilting to advantage in "Tokyo Blues." She outlined the pattern her manufactured strip pattern created as it went from row to row. This caused a slight relief that accentuated to advantage the linear quality of the design. (See Photo 38.)

Decorative quilting with contrasting thread can unite parts of your garment. Cathie Hoover used red machine stitching across minor navy areas of "Red Knots" (Photo 39). The fabric was a simple, delicate stripe that was definitely subordinate to the high activity, woven areas of her garment. The stitching, perpendicular to the direction of the printed stripes, helped to "push up" the activity level of the minor areas. It also diffused the red color from the exuberantly colored woven areas.

EMBELLISHMENTS

Since stripe fabric is patterned, embellishment will most likely have to be done on plain fabric incorporated into the design of the garment if it is to show.

Sashiko Embroidery

Sashiko embroidery is particularly appropriate to use with Japanese stripes, though it could also be used with other types of stripes. There are a number of good books and articles available on how to do sashiko. It's also possible to mail order plastic sashiko patterns and sashiko thread. Consult the Bibliography and Appendix for resources.

I developed a quick version of sashiko to embellish a horizontal panel on the major front of "Akasaka" (Color Plate 41). The pattern, a regular plastic quilting pattern available commercially, called for one line of stitching which I did with large stitches using DMC perle cotton thread #5. It's similar to sashiko thread in weight, but with a luster the real thing lacks. Then I added another line of stitching when the design wasn't bold enough to show on the printed fabric. As another option, I could have also switched to a solid fabric which would have made my design easier to read.

Since there are so many commercial quilting templates available, be particularly careful in selecting one—make sure it matches your stripe in feeling. For example, hearts and flowers would have been wrong with my Japanese stripes.

Sashiko designs fill bands nicely, and can also be used as filler on minor areas or to embellish plain sleeves. Since the stitches are large, consider the kind of wear the area of the garment will receive.

Photo 40. Symbols and Stripes. Grace France, Belgrade, MT

Silk Screen

Grace France used her own original silk screen designs to embellish her garment "Symbols and Stripes" (Photo 40). This is a good way to personalize a creation or carry out a theme or mood. Stenciling can also be used in the same way.

Fabric Manipulation

Lisa Walser embellishes her garments with fabric knots; they add nice surface interest, something that catches your eye upon closer examination. (See Photo 41.) Look closely at Cathie Hoover's vest (Photos 25 and 39) to see another example of this idea.

The knots are made from narrow strips of fabric stitched and turned with a loop turner. They can be cut from straight or bias fabric. The ends of the loops are caught in the seam stitching so they are held permanently in place.

Photo 41. Tailored Knots and Stripes (detail).
Lisa Walser, Missoula, MT

5

GENERAL
SUPPLY
INFORMATION

In this chapter I cover some of the general interest questions about supplies which always come up in my wearables workshops. Students seem to enjoy hearing about a teacher's personal preferences!

PATTERNS

It is as important to have a pattern collection as it is to have a fabric collection. No rational seamstress ever expects to use up all her fabric, so why should she feel guilty if she doesn't use every pattern she owns? Extra patterns offer the same advantages that stacks of fabric do...something to compare and audition against, a last chance in case your first choice doesn't meet expectations, a starting point for those late-night inspirations when the stores are closed.

A word of caution: "style ease" changes over time. Be wary of patterns that have been in your collection too long. They may be too tight or too loose in appearance according to the current fashion look. This is a good reason to make up your selection first in an old sheet or muslin. There are patterns in my collection that I have used a number of times over the years and I consider them "classics." However, every time I use one, I still subject it to a re-evaluation which includes trying on the previous garment to see if we still fit each other.

I most often use commercial patterns for my decorative garments rather than patterns designed specifically for quilters. There are a number of reasons for this very personal decision. Since I generally stick to one company, I feel more confident I will pick the correct size. I usually find the silhouette, cut, and detailing of commercial patterns more interesting, too. These patterns tend to be more flattering in their fit because they have subtle shaping added that patterns designed by quilters often lack. (After taking pattern drafting and French draping in graduate school, I don't mind paying Issey Miyake for his design expertise!) Vogue is my favorite, but I check out all the companies at least twice a year when I compile a "suitable pattern" list for my workshops.

If a pattern really catches my eye, I add it to my collection even though I may not have immediate plans for it. You never know how long patterns will be on the market. Supposedly, the patterns are available from the pattern company for six months after they've been pulled, so if you see one you like but discover it was recently dropped, contact the company directly.

Incidentally, a hint that a pattern is on the way out, or may have reached the end of its life expectancy, is that it appears at the end of its section in the pattern book rather than at the beginning. Another hint: it's shown on a page with several other patterns rather than having a page all to itself.

Where should you look in a commercial pattern book for possible candidates for wearable art? Vests are usually included with blouses. I also peruse the sections of suits and coats and sportswear for possible jackets. Additionally, I check out the designer areas for interesting tops. Don't forget that a vest or interesting top may be part of an ensemble. This means the pattern will cost more, but it's worth it to find an exciting new shape. When vest patterns are scarce, I've been known to adapt a blouse pattern. The pattern Pam Quan used for "Samurai Stripes" was adapted from a blouse pattern.

Some quilters' patterns are available that my students have enjoyed using. Sizing among the independents may vary even more than in the commercial patterns. Check for "boxiness." Is there excess fabric in the vest or jacket back so that it pooches out? Remember this will only be accentuated when batting is added.

When I analyze a pattern, what I'm looking for is the basic garment silhouette and the shape of the individual pieces. Most often simple shapes are best. If a garment is made of many pieces, it is suitable only when all those pieces can fit into your overall piecing design.

I watch for unusual patterns that will help me create a more interesting wearable. A number of the garments featured in this book open asymmetrically. This beginning structure makes it easy to design fronts that don't have to match, that is, fronts with major and minor design areas. Do remember, however, they will have to be worn closed to look good.

When considering specific areas of the garment, the neckline is always important. Will it transfer easily to a quilted version? Generally, collarless garments are the best bet. If there are sleeves that will be quilted, how full are they? Are they set-in, dropped, or raglan? Sleeve design makes a big difference since batting, lining, and bindings are part of the finished project.

When selecting a pattern, individual figures and personal preferences should not be overlooked. For example, large-busted women find V-necks more flattering, and generally dislike any excess fabric that creates folds between the bustline and armhole edge. This frequently happens in garments based on ethnic patterns where rectangular, rather than curved, shapes are used.

Unless you look closely, what you see may not be what you get as far as selecting a pattern is concerned. Fashion photographs are helpful because they show the garment on real people, even if they are models who are never too big-hipped or full-breasted. However, even with photographs, it's often difficult to determine how the garment is constructed, where the seams are, or more importantly, whether there are darts. For this reason, fashion illustrations may be more informative. I also find the little line drawings of the front and back views very useful.

To estimate the amount of "fashion" ease in a pattern, read the verbal description. Be wary of phrases such as "loose fitting" and "very loose fitting." Sandra Betzina, author of *Power Sewing*, suggests purchasing a size smaller pattern if you see the words "very loose fitting." (One reason I prefer Vogue patterns is they give the most detailed descriptions. Some of the other companies use the minimum amount of descriptive words.) Another way to check for fullness: find the section on the yardage chart that gives the widths at the lower edge for each size, then compare this with your hip measurement.

Pattern Size

Unfortunately, pattern size does not necessarily correspond to ready-made size. We all know that if you're willing to pay more for a ready-made, you often can squeeze into a smaller size.

Check your measurements periodically; alas, they do change over the years. Some women continue to buy the same size pattern even though their body may have changed dramatically. They end up having to add so much to the pattern with adjustments that it would be a lot easier to just buy a larger size to begin with. Psychologically, this is hard to do, but when the garment is finished, only you know what size pattern you used.

For commercial patterns, Sandra Betzina suggests determining your high bust measurement and substituting it for the bust measurement when selecting a size. (To determine your high bust measurement, place the tape under your armpits and high on the bust rather than across the fullest part of the bust.) The hardest to fit area of the body is the upper chest area. If your pattern fits there, any adjustments needed will occur at the side seams where it's much easier to add additional inches.

If you're using patterns for quilters, you will have to estimate your size. Happily all sizes are usually printed on the same piece of paper, so you'll actually have all the sizes available if you guess wrong.

To make sure you've selected the correct size pattern (whether commercial or quilters'), check your measurements against those of the pattern. Begin with your bust measurement measured in the traditional way across the fullest part of the bust. Think about how tight you like your clothes. Consider what you will be wearing under a vest or jacket. A lightweight blouse? A bulky turtleneck sweater? Add a minimum of 1½" to 2" to your full bust measure to include the wearing ease. Compare this measurement against the circumference of your pattern.

As you check your bust measurement against the pattern measurements, there are several other things to consider. If the garment is a vest or coat, do the front edges meet, overlap, or end a few inches apart? (Consult the fashion illustration to make sure.) This makes a difference when you compare your measurements against the pattern measurements. Remember to subtract the seam allowances from the pattern pieces when checking the measurements. Often seam allowances aren't printed on the pattern, and if you don't catch this common mistake, you may end up with less room than you expected. If using a quilters' pattern, trace your choice and keep the original pattern for future reference.

The average American woman is one to two sizes bigger on the bottom half of her figure. Patterns for vests and jackets should be selected to fit the high bust area, as just discussed, but if you are typical, you may need to add additional circumference if the garment reaches to the hips.

Fitting Tips

I find it essential to first make up a decorative garment in an old sheet or "ugly" fabric to see if I'm going in the right direction. It's a shame to spend a lot of time creating and then discover that the project doesn't fit very well or that it's unflattering. I use a machine-basting stitch so I can easily rip out stitches if necessary. Backstitch at the end of seams so your work stays together long enough for you to try it on several times.

To make it easier to judge the pattern, cut away the seam allowances at the neck, the armholes, and around the edges of vests and jackets so you can see where the true edge really is in the finished garment. Make

Figure 5-1.
Check shoulder.

A. Extend shoulder and
redraw.

B. Check lower armhole and
possibly redraw, too.

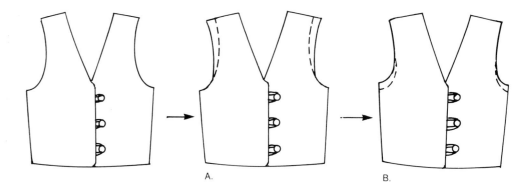

A.   B.

changes right on the fabric and then, if they work, transfer your changes to the tissue or paper pattern. Let me caution you against just holding up or pinning together the tissue or paper pattern. Fabric really makes a difference. It drapes over the body contours far better than paper. When you're eager to get started on the real thing, the time spent making this pre-garment may seem a waste. Not true! You only have to skip this step once, labor long and hard on a garment, then have it be all wrong for you—you'll never skip this again when making a wearable.

Here are some areas to check for possible pattern changes or adjustments when making quilted, decorative clothing:

1. Check the neckline. You may want to lower it so it won't rub you. If there are many piecing seams plus the batting and binding, it will probably be stiff at the edge. If your garment is part of an outfit, think about what kind of blouse or shirt will be underneath. Turtlenecks and blouses with collars provide a protective soft padding to protect your neck. They also help the garment stay fresh longer because they keep the neck area clean.

2. On a vest, you may want to enlarge the armhole slightly by cutting it out at the lower front so it won't cut into you. It depends on what kind of sleeve you plan to wear with your vest. There's a tremendous difference between the sleeves of a classic cotton turtleneck and some of the fashionable big sleeves popular in blouses today. It's a good idea to put on the actual garment while fitting your vest. If the blouse will include shoulder pads, make sure they are in place because they do take up room. (For the same reason, if you are making a jacket, vest, or top that will have shoulder pads, make sure they are pinned in.)

3. Check the shoulder area on vests. Extended shoulders give a larger canvas to design on so you may want to consider redrawing the area by

pinning on a small strip of fabric and reshaping the armhole. Even if you think you have large shoulders, extended shoulders are often flattering. To experiment with this, just extend the shoulder an inch or so and redraw the armhole edge (Figure 5-1). The armhole will end up being smaller in total circumference because the shoulder is sloped, so check this addition by trying on the vest. Make necessary minor corrections such as cutting out the bottom of the armhole so your sleeve can flow freely.

4. If you have drag lines (unwanted folds of fabric) in garments where the bodice and sleeve are cut as one, try inserting shoulder pads. This works particularly well for busty women.

5. Where does the bottom edge of a vest (or jacket) hit on your body? Is it flattering? Does it divide your silhouette in a pleasing way? You'd be surprised how much difference a half-inch or an inch can make. Often quilters want to cover and hide their stomach and hips, but shorter tops present simpler design surfaces to fill.

6. How does the garment sit on your body? Because many vests designed specifically for quilters are squareish, they tend to pooch out at the center back. Commercial patterns are more apt to have subtle curves and shaping added. To correct boxiness, the back side seams can be slanted in from the armhole to the bottom, perhaps half an inch on each side (Figure 5-2). Though squared shapes are easier to fill with patchwork, opt for a shaped area that fits the body nicely. The viewer's eye will be more aware of what is happening center front and center back. The side seams are often obscured by the arm anyway.

7. Small amounts of extra fabric can cause the garment to stand away from the body (Figure 5-3). Watch especially for the front on a V-neck in the upper chest area, and the front armhole. Small 1/8" tucks will ease this out and can be transfered to the tissue where they are

pleated out and taped or pinned. Then just pat away the fullness as it goes into the pattern proper. Essentially, you're decreasing the circumference of the edge. One, two, or, at the most, three small tucks do the trick. Remember to consider the sleeve that will be worn with the garment; often it camouflages this extra fullness and you don't even have to worry about it.

8. Check the hip area if your vest or jacket is a longer version and you have larger hips. Don't switch to a bigger size pattern to fit the hips better. It is more important to get a good fit for your top half. Most often you can add extra width at the bottom of the side seams and then redraw the cutting line between the bust and the bottom edge of the garment, making sure the shaping is gradual. Divide the amount needed to be added between the four seams (Figure 5-4).

Figure 5-2.
To reduce boxiness, take in back side seams by moving them in ½" and redrawing.

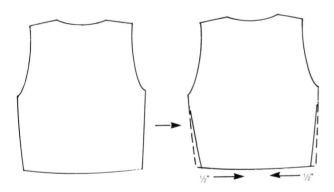

Figure 5-3.
To reduce fullness on V-neck and/or front armhole, make small ⅛" tucks.

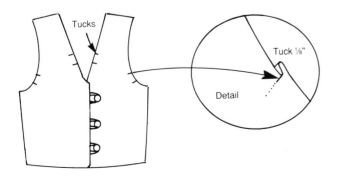

Figure 5-4.
Increasing hip size of long vest or jacket.

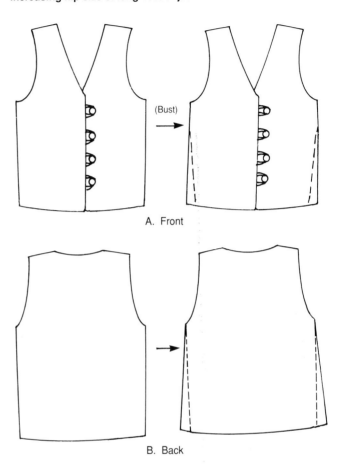

A. Front

B. Back

SELECTING MATERIALS

Though many varied materials are used in creating wearables, again I have my personal recommendations and preferences.

Fabric

The majority of the fabric used in constructing the garments illustrated in this book was 100% cotton. It's much easier to piece 100% cotton than cotton/poly blends because there's less stretch. Many silk and silk-like fabrics require extra special care in handling. For a first project, I would certainly suggest 100% cotton. Don't make life any more difficult than necessary.

Lining and Bindings

Pieced garments need to be lined to cover and protect the small seams. If they are quilted like a quilt, a backing is necessary and it acts as the lining. I usually prefer to quilt through the top and batting only. Then I add a separate lining which covers the batting. It hangs separately and produces a more finished look to the inside.

You may want to select your lining material at the same time you select the other fabrics to be used. It can be plain and merely coordinated by color, or lining can be an opportunity to make one more design statement. I usually prefer the latter approach. You may argue that no one else will see it; I would counter that *you* will see it. To me, it's a little like the red slip that my mother bought me when I was a poor graduate student. I knew it was there, and it made me feel wonderful.

If you opt for a wilder approach to your lining, coordinate it in some way to what's going on in the garment —don't just use leftovers. Sometimes people do get glimpses of it as the garment moves on your body. Besides, you may end up wanting to hang your piece in a show, and then everyone will see what you have put inside.

What type of lining fabric is best? Obviously, it should be compatible with your other fabrics. If you are hand or machine quilting through it, select it just as you would the back of a quilt. If it will be separate, you have other options. While I always end up with cotton, some people prefer a slicker surface so the garment will slide off and on more easily. This feature is particularly nice in heavier coats and jackets, or any garment where sleeves are involved. Keep in mind that these slick synthetics will require drycleaning and are warmer to wear.

Many quilted garments use binding to finish the edge or cover the inside seams. I use scraps from my "fashion" fabrics (the fabrics that show on the outside) or lining pieces for this purpose. I find these scraps far superior to purchased bias tape. Allow for bindings when you estimate the yardage required for a finished garment. For example, I often purchase an extra one-half yard of lining.

Sewing and Quilting Thread

This is a controversial issue, but I only use cotton thread on my sewing machine. Years ago I was told by a sewing-machine repairman that polyester threads build up static electricity in the tension mechanism which causes skipped stitches. Since switching, I've never had this problem again.

It is often difficult to pick a thread color when a garment has many different colors. I generally select as neutral a thread color as possible—something with a middle value, perhaps just past dark beige or a medium gray. If the contrast of values is high, for example black and white, I select the darker color. If I were using red and navy fabric, I'd pick navy thread. The idea is to see the thread as little as possible.

Be careful of the color of your basting thread. White, pastels, or neutrals are best. Often basting is seen as an opportunity to use up old thread, but dark thread may "crock" or rub off its color when pulled out. This could be disastrous on a light surface.

Some people make pieced garments and don't quilt them. To me this is courting disaster. I'm happiest when there is at least some attachment to a foundation batting. When selecting a thread color for quilting, consider whether you want your stitching to show or not. If you decide to use hand quilting, you may want to showcase your stitching. Pick a hue or value that will be more visible. Often machine quilting, particularly when done in the ditch, is best if it shows the least.

In fact, this may be the perfect time to try machine quilting if you haven't yet experimented with it since the areas to be filled are small. I use regular 100% cotton mercerized thread on top and in the bobbin. You may opt for the invisible nylon thread used in the machine quilting of quilts. This is teamed with regular cotton thread in the bobbin. (The stiff quilting thread coated with silicone is for hand quilting only.)

Batting

Not all pieced garments have a batting, but many do. Batting adds both more protection and some body to the garment. When deciding on batting, a major concern is the loft, or puffiness, of the batt. Personal preferences, loftwise, vary considerably. Some quilters prefer a batt which produces surface relief so there's a noticeable difference between quilted and unquilted areas. Others feel this "puffy" effect adds optical pounds and prefer the look of a flatter surface.

The quilt batting companies have developed batts which can be used in clothing. These polyester batts are categorized as "low loft." Used as they come, or split in half so they will be even thinner, they produce a surface that shows a surface contrast between stitched and unstitched areas.

Batts that are 100% cotton or 80% cotton/20% polyester produce a flatter surface than the all-polyester batts. They're also easier to work with if you want to machine quilt the garment. Many years ago, Virginia Avery taught me that cotton batts can be right next to the feed dogs and won't get caught. Machine quilt through your pieced top and batting. The lining can then be set in later.

I generally use outing flannel inside my garments. It produces a flat surface that contours very nicely to the body. I have always preferred the flat look of old quilts and find the same effect pleasing in garments. Outing flannel is also easy to hand or machine quilt, and it's the coolest to wear in warm weather.

Closures

Interesting closures can provide the perfect finishing touch for your garment. This may be the time for a splurge if you can find just the right button or toggle. Bead shops, specialty shops that carry buttons, or antique stores that have clothing are good places to look.

Decorative gripper snaps applied to a band are another possibility. Sometimes self-covered buttons or a self-tie is sufficient. If you want to simplify the surface, large covered snaps or the flat hooks and eyes used for skirt waistbands may be adequate. They are the most attractive when attached with a neatly done buttonhole stitch.

SELECTING EQUIPMENT

Out on the prairie, quilters made do. They used what they had and made wonderful quilts. Today we have a plethora of gadgets and tools to help us be better quilters. How many of them do we really need? My answer is, "If what you have works fine, great, but if you are having problems, start shopping around." Happily, we don't have to make do anymore, but all the gadgets in the world won't help unless you sit down and do the sewing.

Drafting Tools

Many quilters get into fancy drafting pencils. An ordinary #2 pencil works fine for me. However, make sure you have a good pencil sharpener, and use it. Big, fat lines are not accurate. For pencils for marking fabric, see the following section on "Cutting and Marking Equipment."

Like many other quilters, I have used See-thru rulers for years. Recently, I also learned to use the wonderful new Omnigrid rulers for drafting designs as well as cutting fabric. See the following section for more information on these clever tools.

Cutting and Marking Equipment

You can make no better investment than a good pair of shears. Personally, I think Ginghers are the best. Though more expensive than many other brands, they will bring you pleasure far exceeding the cost. To prolong the sharp blades on your good cutting shears, don't get into the habit of clipping sewing machine threads with them; use a small pair of scissors or a clipper for this task. (Continually using the same 2" blade area for cutting threads will dull the blades over time. Eventually this becomes very noticeable when you have a hard time cutting the material at the end of your cutting stroke.)

A rotary cutter and mat—I prefer the Olfa brand—can speed up many cutting tasks. Practice is necessary to become accurate so prepare to sacrifice a little fabric from your collection. It's best to practice *before* you begin a project, rather than *on* a project.

My favorite rulers to use with the rotary cutter are the Omnigrid brand. These high-quality rulers are marked in two colors, yellow and dark green, making it possible to read the lines against a wide variety of fabric colors. Attention left-handers: Omnigrid rulers are marked so they can be read and used from either direction. They come in a variety of sizes, but good starting sizes for wearables are the 3" x 18" and the 6" square.

I don't like marking fabric with ink pens. I'm afraid some part of the line will remain after cutting and later bleed when I press my work. If I'm marking on dark fabrics, I use Verithin silver pencils, available at quilt stores or art supply stores.

I prefer plastic template material, the kind that's cloudy white and rougher on one side than the other. I select a medium-gauge thickness so I can cut the plastic with an old pair of shears. Personally, the printed, grided template material is bothersome; the lines are never where I want them to be.

If you are tracing individual templates on your fabric, it is necessary to have a slightly rough surface underneath so the fabric won't stretch and distort. If you don't have a rotary cutting mat, cover a piece of cardboard with fine sandpaper. Tape around the edges to finish it off and to hold the sandpaper in place.

I mustn't forget one of my most necessary tools, my seam ripper. Yes, I still rip! (My high school students always found great comfort in this confession.) Believe it or not, I have the same seam ripper I had in the 5th grade, and it is still sharp.

Glendora Hutson, who taught me precision piecing, always said, "Rip once for you and once for me; more than that is up to you." If I can't get it right after two tries, I usually give up. If it is really crucial, I might try one more time, but that is definitely it. Some of the stitching I do isn't perfect, but the majority of it is pretty good. After all, a human hand guided the machine.

Irons and Pressing Equipment

A good iron is another essential. The more holes on the sole plate, the more steam comes out and the better pressing job you can do. I prefer a "shot of steam" feature. Learn to press as you go. A small portable ironing board near your machine can save much getting up and walking across the room to press small pieces. I love the Portapress board which is available by mail order. Consult the Appendix for address information.

Sewing Machine Equipment

Though garments in this book were constructed by sewing machine, it isn't necessary to have a fancy machine to create wearables. Most of my sewing is done on my grandmother's Singer Featherweight portable which is over 50 years old.

Sewing machines with even feed attachments make it easier to machine quilt. If you don't have the attachment, see if your local sewing machine dealer can order one. (Warning: These are only for machines which can zigzag. They don't mesh properly with the feed dogs of straight-stitching machines.)

Sergers are used to finish the unbound seams in unquilted, unlined garments. They can also be used to finish off ribbed bands.

Not all sewing pins are alike. I prefer the Illse pins because they are quite long. (They're available from the Cotton Patch; check the Appendix for the address.) If I can't get the Illse pins, I also use the long ones with the glass heads. The extra length gives me something to hold onto when I'm sending small pieces through the sewing machine.

Viewing Items

Some wearables creators like the three-dimensional aspect of working on a mannequin, but even pinning the pieces on a quilt pin-up wall will be helpful for viewing purposes. (This is much safer than leaving them strewn across the floor while you contemplate them.) A place to display your work-in-progress also allows you to "visit" the project from time to time throughout the day. These mini-viewings help keep you thinking about the project. Your right brain may be working on a wonderful solution to surprise you with in the morning!

Worktables

Worktables are important, too, so you can spread out your project. Sewing machines in cabinets don't have enough workspace for me. My corner arrangement of two tables, each 30" x 60", provides room to spread out parts of the garment as I piece. I can also swivel my secretarial chair to the right and do pressing on the second table.

In addition, I have a stand-up worktable; standing up lets me change positions so I'm not so stiff from long hours of sewing. My table has an adjustable height and can be disassembled and put away if need be. Unfortunately, this model is no longer available, but Doug and Sandy, formally Seth Products, are marketing two new lines of tables called "A-Just-A-Table Systems." Consult the Appendix for the address of Uni-Unique Products.

While it's not essential to have a studio to construct quilts or wearables, it surely helps to have a special place set up, ready to go, all the time. In that way, small pieces of free time can be utilized.

CARE OF FABRIC AND GARMENT

I prewash my fabric in my washing machine even though I generally dryclean my finished garments. Prewashing rinses out excess dye and removes sizing. This makes the fabric softer and easier to hand quilt.

The one exception is chintz fabric. Most often I use it as is because the shine is one of the main reasons I purchased it. If you must prewash it, don't put it in the dryer. Additional shine may be lost.

Subjecting a pieced garment to the rigors of the washing machine exposes it to the maximum stress. Though drycleaning is less stressful, some people don't like the chemical odors. (I allow time for airing outside.) Either use the best drycleaner in town or carefully hand launder.

If you are considering hand washing a garment, ask yourself if you will be able to press it easily after it is washed. Special effects such as biscuit puffs and cordings that are placed close together are very difficult to press with any degree of success after they have been washed.

Vests, jackets, and coats will need less cleaning than dresses and blouses because they are worn over other garments. Keep this in mind when deciding what kind of garment to make.

6

CONSTRUCTION
TECHNIQUES

The actual construction of a garment may not be as exciting and exhilarating as designing it, but there is alot of satisfaction in a job well done. Good workmanship is unobtrusive. Good craft helps to showcase your design ideas.

PRECISION TECHNIQUES

I love to sew and by nature can't seem to help being a picky perfectionist. On the other hand, accuracy may not be so important to you. That doesn't mean that you can't enjoy making wearables. In does mean in selecting a prospective wearables project, you must consider your own skill level. Match your expectations with what you can do, but always stretch a little and try new things. When I graded garments, part of the grade was for effort expended.

Further, if workmanship skills are keeping you from doing some of the things you think you might enjoy, work on improving them. My basic philosophy is, "If you want your piecing to be accurate, you simply have to *be* accurate." That means accuracy in drafting, cutting, pinning, stitching, and pressing.

The key word is, of course, "accuracy." If you are inaccurate in any of these steps, you may not get the results you had in mind. The other key word is "want." If the desire is there, you can do it. The process has to upstage the product for awhile, however. Many beginners "generate" rather than "compose" projects, using as many fast methods as they can find. I'm not saying you can't use fast methods. But be aware of the process and the goal, not just the product and the clock.

Learning to Draft Accurately

All 2" squares are not alike. Some are drawn accurately, some aren't. Take time to really draw what you want, rather than being haphazard and making do. Being a little off may not be so awful when you are working on a large scale, but small pieces are far less forgiving.

Once you have drawn an accurate geometric shape on graph paper, make sure you do a good job of adding a real ¼" seam allowance. This isn't so hard when the edges are either vertical or horizontal: just draw on the line that is ¼" away from your first line. Trouble comes with drawing diagonal seam allowances.

If you just line up the red line on your See-thru ruler with the diagonal and draw, your seam allowance will be more than ¼" wide because you added in the width of the lead. Instead, try the following:

1. Back up your ruler a tad before you draw your line. The ¼" red line will be just behind, not on top of, your pencil line (see Figure 6-1).
2. Draw the line very carefully, making sure to maintain an even width.
3. Check your accuracy by moving the See-thru ruler so your first and second pencil lines register with two red lines in the middle of the ruler. If you can't see your pencil lines underneath the red lines, it means you have done a good job of adding an accurate ¼" seam allowance.
4. If you can see your pencil lines, meaning they don't line up with the red lines, you need to erase and try again. Many quilters draft and add seam allowances inaccurately. If you are machine piecing, this will cause you grief; hand piecers can cheat a little and often get themselves out of such a predicament. However, their tops aren't always flat when they are finished.

Marking Corners

If your piecing is straightforward, it isn't necessary to mark the exact position of the corners. However, if you get into unusual geometric shapes, you will find it helpful to have a registration mark to line up two pieces before stitching.

When you trace and cut your template, mark the unusual or odd corners on the plastic at the same time. While you are tracing your pieces or after you cut them,

Figure 6-1.
To add accurate ¼" seam allowance:

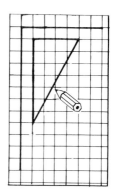

A. Draw triangle. Add seam allowance to right-angle sides.

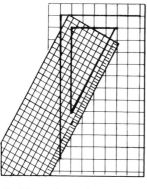

B. Place ruler ¼" from diagonal edge.

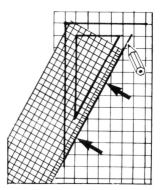

C. Move back slightly to allow for pencil lead width. Draw.

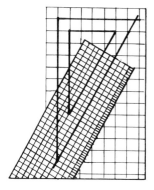

D. Check accuracy by lining up two lines in the middle of the ruler.

transfer the corner marking to the *wrong* side of the fabric pieces. There are several ways to do this; here's the method I use for marking as I go:

1. Trace the template onto the wrong side of the fabric (Figure 6-2).
2. Position the pencil right above the corner dot on the template.
3. Quickly pull the template away, and put the pencil straight down on the fabric. Mark.
4. Slide the template back into position and check the accuracy of the dot.

If you have a small awl, you can use it to make a marking hole in your template, if you prefer. It's also possible to order a quarter-punch at a stationery store. This makes a smaller hole than regular paper punches.

One word of caution: when working with oddly shaped pieces, keep track of the right and wrong side when you are cutting them from solid fabric. Oddly shaped pieces only fit one way—they are not interchangeable as some simple geometric shapes are.

Figure 6-2.
To mark corner dot:

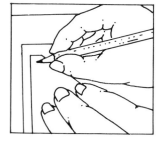

A. Position pencil above dot.

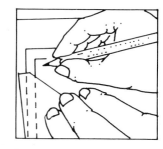

B. Pull template away and place pencil down.

I also mark the right side of my templates with a number. This not only helps me keep track of the right and wrong sides, it also keeps me from confusing similarly shaped pieces. Masking tape makes a good surface to write numbers on.

Precision Machine Sewing

Learn to become good friends with your sewing machine. I love the one I do my piecing on because it belonged to my grandmother; it's older than I am. It is one of those old black, Singer Featherweight portables that quilters so cherish. It stitches forwards and backwards. That is all that it does, but it does it very well.

Problems with Zigzag Machines

Perhaps you have a fancier machine. Maybe it also zigzags. Though this is an added bonus for some things, it isn't an added bonus for straight stitching accurate ¼" seams. Several things can cause problems.

The throat plate has an opening for the needle to go up and down through as it catches the bobbin thread (Figure 6-3). The hole is made wider when the machine zigzags so that the needle can also go back and forth from side to side. The increased size of the hole makes

Figure 6-3.
Sewing machine throat plates.

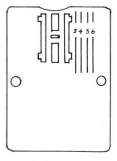

A. Zigzag.

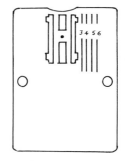

B. Straight stitch.

it easier to catch up your fabric when you begin your stitching. It's possible to order a straight stitching throat plate for most machines. The smaller hole doesn't suck up the fabric. However, you must be very careful to not turn the dial to zigzag while this plate is in place, or you will break the needle.

Changing the throat plate on a zigzag machine helps, but it is impossible to change where the feed dogs are positioned. You can't move them closer together like they are on a straight-stitching machine. Your fabric may not want to feed through as easily as it does on the straight stitcher. Sometimes a long pin or seam ripper can be used to help guide your fabric through. Even on my Featherweight, I do this when I am sending the long, unwieldy tails of triangles through the presser foot.

Calibrating Your Sewing Machine

Most machines do not have a mark on the throat plate where ¼" is. If you want to sew accurately, you need to know where this is. "Eyeballing" won't do. Many sewers assume the edge of their presser foot is ¼", but this is seldom true.

Follow these directions (and see Figure 6-4) to accurately calibrate your machine:

1. Place a See-thru ruler under the feed dogs. Put the needle right into the ¼" line. Lower the presser foot.
2. Place a piece of masking or Dymo tape next to the ruler. Bring the needle up, raise the presser foot, and set aside the ruler.
3. To check that your tape is accurately placed, sew along a piece of graph paper. First, evenly cut the edge off the graph paper to make sure you have a long accurate line at the edge.
4. Sew the piece of graph paper through your machine, being careful to keep the just-cut edge up against the edge of the tape. Focus here—don't worry about the ¼" line.
5. Now check the graph paper. If the stitching is right on top of the ¼" line, you've done a good job; if it isn't, go back to Step 1 and try again.
6. If you have used masking tape, build up the tape with several pieces so a ridge is formed to run your fabric against.

The masking tape ridge will need to be renewed occasionally. Check it from time to time to make sure you are still sewing accurately. I use a long piece of masking tape so I can get a running start, so to speak. When you are first learning to sew more precisely, periodically check your seams. Hold one under a See-thru ruler and see if the stitching line and edge of the fabric line up with two red lines ¼" apart.

Figure 6-4.
To calibrate sewing machine for ¼" seam allowance:

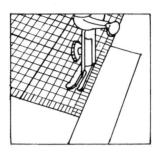

A. Position ruler and run tape along ruler ¼" from needle.

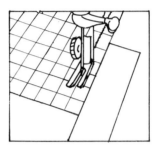

B. Stitch on graph paper.

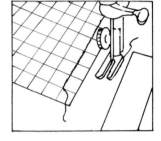

C. Check for accuracy.

All machines may not be as easy to mark as mine is. On some machines, it may be necessary to break the tape so the throat plate can be opened to get to the bobbin. Wide zigzag feed dogs may also be placed where you should be placing your marking tape. In this case, you will have to run the tape up to the hole for the feed dogs and stop.

General Sewing Tips

I find these general sewing rules helpful for piecing patchwork:

1. Always place the pins with the heads *away* from the edge. This is most likely just the reverse of the method you learned in dress-making, but you don't want to accidentally try to sew over the heads.
2. When pinning two pieces of fabric together, always pin the two ends first. Then place a pin in the middle. More pins can be added, if necessary, after these three are in place. If there is any fullness, divide it evenly.
3. Leave your pins in while you are sewing patch-work. They help to hold the pieces in place. I press down on them with my fingers if I'm having trouble sending the piece through the presser foot and feed dogs in a straight path.
4. If for some unknown reason, one of the two pieces to be sewn together seems larger than it should be, pin the fabrics together, the

largest side on the bottom. Evenly distribute the fullness. Sew the seam with the fullest side next to the feed dogs, as you send the fabric through. They will work to ease in the extra fullness.

5. Learn where to look when you sew. Look at the tape when sewing ¼" seams; look at the needle for other stitching such as machine quilting on drawn lines.

Pressing

I was always taught to press as I went along in a project, in fact to never stitch across a seam unless it had been pressed first. Sometimes we get lazy and don't want to take the time to do this. Part of this reluctance has to do with the inconvenience of having to stop one process and start something else. Having a small pressing station right next to your sewing machine will encourage you to press more frequently.

If what I am doing is very small scale, I occasionally will allow myself to fingerpress. To do this, use the edge of your thumbnail to crease the area to be flattened. I drag the nail along the seam line, holding the seam allowance underneath, in the direction I want it to go. Once the unit is completed, I press it with an iron.

Incidentally, there actually is a difference between pressing and ironing. Basically, ironing is a scrubbing motion, to remove wrinkles. Pressing is an up and down motion, to set seams in place.

In patchwork, the ¼" seams are most often pressed to one side rather than pressed open. This makes them stronger. I often fingerpress the seam to get it started. Then I bring my iron in from the side without the seam allowance as I set it down (Figure 6-5). This helps to truly flatten the seam. If you come straight down from above, as in pressing seams open, you may end up with a slight fold or tuck, rather than a flat seam. Keep checking as you go along. When the seam has been pressed perfectly, give it a shot of steam to reinforce what you have done.

One last hint: I always press my pieces into a terry cloth towel. The resilience of the towel helps absorb the weight of the iron and cushions the double seam allowance. If you follow this procedure, you will find that your seam allowances don't show so much from the right side.

PREPARING AND ASSEMBLING INDIVIDUAL GARMENT PIECES

When the garment has been fully adjusted for fit, I cut out the individual pieces in the batting I have selected. Beginning with my original paper pattern which has had any adjustments added, I pin the pieces in place. It's

Figure 6-5.
To press seam:

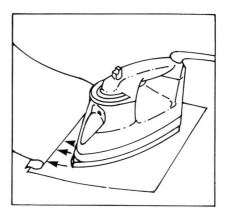

A. Come in from side with sideways motion.

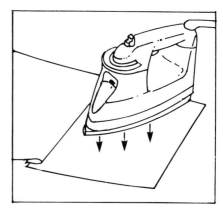

B. Press iron down.

important to allow for a fudge factor here. As I cut out each piece, I add an additional ¼" to all the edges. (If the lining is to be quilted with the pieced top, add ¼" as you cut it, too. If the lining will be separate, cut it the normal way, without the additional ¼".)

I now have a foundation for my designing, a guide for the space I need to fill. Pieces, or groups of pieces, may be stitched directly onto this foundation/batting, or the separate pieces may be individually constructed and joined to the batting when they are hand or machine quilted. Either way, now I have a guide for the amount of patchwork I'll need to create.

After each piece has been quilted, I use my original pattern to true-up the finished piece. Sometimes the quilting process has made it smaller and most of the ¼" that was originally added will be gone. Other times, the excess remains and needs to be cut off.

Remember, the viewer's eye will be most aware of what is happening at the center front and less aware of what is happening at the side seams. Make sure the center is perfect, all your triangles have their points, etc. No one will notice if there are partial units at the underarm seam. Another area that the eye automatically goes to is the bottom edge. Try to have things consistent here.

In creating wearable art, we often design individual parts that will eventually go together to create a whole garment piece. Sometimes in the frenzy of creativity, we don't work out the mechanics of how they will all magically fit together.

An all-over ground plan of what can be joined to what is helpful. Try to organize your small segments into larger shapes which can then be sewn together. Sometimes it will be necessary to add some filler to make this possible.

Repetitive Designs

Throughout this book, we've discussed two basic methods for designing a pieced garment. In the first, a series of different blocks, or repetitive designs, is created. Multiples of each block are then pieced and arranged in a row. Individual blocks can vary slightly in size, but since they are joined to like blocks it doesn't make a difference as long as the rows are the same over-all length. "Amtrak-Am-Slow" and "A Stripe Is a Stripe, Is a Stripe" are good examples of this procedure. In these garments, individual rows were joined to form larger segments which could then be joined to fill a whole pattern piece.

Creating All-over Grids

In the second approach, the size unit is decided on and stays constant throughout the project so it is easy to sew together. There may be more than one block or module used, but they can all be easily mixed or joined in a specific pattern when sewn because they form a grid. All the blocks could be pieced as the modules in "Eucalyptus" or "Cover Stripes" are. Or a set of plain/pieced blocks could be alternated with a specialty block such as a traditional or origami puff, as in "Route 66" and "Sunset: Coast Highway One." In fact, the blocks could all just be plain one-patches of different fabrics. "Akasaka" is made of plain squares cut in different stripes, then laid out to create an optical pattern.

QUILTING

I most often quilt through the decorative top and batting only. I do this in both hand and machine quilting. This is easy to do if you use flannel for hand quilting and flannel or cotton batting for machine quilting.

There are a number of reasons why I prefer this procedure. For one thing, the lining remains neat looking. If you don't have an even feed attachment for your sewing machine, any drag lines caused by the feed dogs pulling the bottom layer through faster than the top one will be hidden on the inside. If you are hand quilting, stitching through two layers rather than three will permit you to make smaller stitches.

Hand and Machine Quilting

I enjoy hand quilting. When I first began, I used a size 7 or 8 needle; I've now worked up to a 9. Size 12 holds no magic for me. They are too hard to thread and bend easily. My stitches are as small as many people's who use a 12, so why should I add frustration to the process?

Since most individual garment pieces are relatively small, they can be hand quilted without a hoop. If your pieces are larger or if you find your stitches have too tight a tension, use a small hoop. I like the "Q Snap" frames made by the Lamb Art Press. You can buy a set which makes an 11" x 17" rectangle. Since the frames are collapsible, they are easy to carry in a quilting bag or suitcase. (See Appendix for address.)

If you are really serious about machine quilting, first read Harriet Hargrave's book, *Heirloom Machine Quilting*. Then buy an even feed attachment for your machine if it is a zigzag model. Find, and take, a class from a good machine quilting teacher. Then practice, and practice some more.

If machine quilting is new to you, start simply. Begin with straight lines to fill in a solid minor area on a garment. I often use straight lines that can be marked with masking tape. You can also try marking lines with a soft

Figure 6-6.
To machine quilt straight lines:

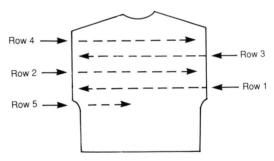

A. Stitch horizontal lines.

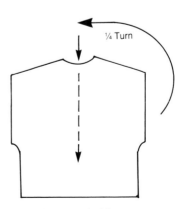

B. Stitch vertical lines.

pencil, a Chalkenor, or a silver or white pencil. If you decide to make a striped project, do machine quilting along the lines of a minor area to attach the piece to the foundation/batting.

Try the following process for machine quilting straight lines:

1. Beginning in the middle section of the pattern piece, start at one edge and sew across to the other edge, stitching right beside the edge of the tape or on the line. (See Figure 6-6.)
2. Turn the fabric around and sew the next line in the opposite direction.
3. When one-half has been completed, return to the center where you began and sew to the opposite edge.
4. If there is both vertical and horizontal quilting, return to the center portion again, rotate the piece a quarter turn, and begin the process again by stitching perpendicular to your first set of lines.
5. If you have to start or stop your machine quilting at other than the edge, thread the end of the thread through a hand sewing needle, pull it through to the back side, and tie it in a knot with the bobbin thread. Wait and do this task after the whole piece has been quilted, rather than stopping and doing it row by row as you go along.

Roz Zinns used this method to machine quilt several grids on "Japanese Mondrian." (See Color Plate 45.) She varied her thread color on different segments for more interest.

Large, all-over grid patterns made from pieced shapes are the easiest to machine quilt. If your pieces are simple shapes that can be joined to form rectangles, they can be sewn together in rows. There are then two ways to machine quilt them to your batting.

Figure 6-7.
To stitch in the ditch, stitch next to the seam line.

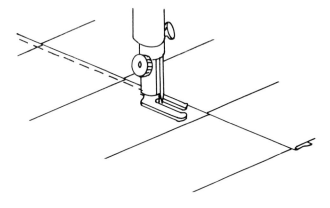

Follow one of the procedures described earlier for sewing your pieces together. Then decide which of the following machine quilting procedures would work the best for you.

Stitching in the Ditch

1. If you would like to "stitch in the ditch" on the right side, baste your completed fabric to the batting. (Some people pin-baste only.)
2. Begin with the middle row of the rows to be stitched and carefully sew in or near the crevice created by the seams being sewn. This is appropriately called "stitching in the ditch." Work on stitching as straight as you can (Figure 6-7).
3. Switch directions as you sew the next row. Move from the center row toward an edge; return to the center area, work to the other edge.

This is the method used in "Akasaka." (See Color Plate 41 for a closeup detail.) I stitched with black thread since black was common to all the stripes used. If the machine stitching line seems too obtrusive, try nylon thread.

Invisible Quilting

If you prefer to not have any machine stitching show, it's possible to attach your pieces to the batting without having it show on the outside. Again, complete the steps described earlier to create a whole piece of fabric from your units, then follow this procedure:

1. Beginning at one of the edges, line up the first row of blocks. Fold the remaining rows back so the first row seam is exposed (Figure 6-8).
2. Pin-baste the row in place to the batting. Guide lines drawn beforehand on the batting are helpful to use as a reference point to keep your rows straight.
3. Re-stitch through your first ¼" seam, stitching this time through the batting as well.
4. From the right side, re-press the seam and front area you have just stitched.
5. Repeat Steps 1 through 4 until all the seams have been stitched in place. Keep checking that you're keeping the seams parallel to the guide lines and that your work is staying neat and flat.

The double stitching of the seams described in Step 3 is efficient in the long run. It is hard for me to combine the stitching of the seam and the stitching to the batting in one step. If I try that method, my seam usually isn't as accurate. This means I waste time ripping and restitching. Therefore, it becomes less frustrating and more efficient to just sew an accurate seam twice, rather than one inaccurate seam that has to be redone.

BINDING AND SEAM FINISHES

If there is very little piecing in your garment, you may be able to line it in a traditional way; just follow the procedure on the pattern guide sheet. However, if you have used a lot of piecing and you will be quilting, the garment will wear better if the seams are individually finished and the edges bound rather than using facings or linings that are stitched to the edge. In that case, follow this procedure:

1. If the lining has been quilted with the top and batting, trim the pieces to size after the quilting has been completed, then proceed to step 5.
2. If you have chosen to quilt only the top and batting together, trim each completed quilted piece to size.
3. Match each piece with its lining piece, making sure the back side of the lining is placed next to the exposed back of the batting.
4. Baste around the edge by hand. I usually pin-baste the two together first. Check to make sure both sides are smooth and wrinkle free.
5. Join the front and back at the shoulder and side seams. You now have a choice of finishing techniques.

Figure 6-8.
Invisible quilting—stitch on top of ¼" seam.

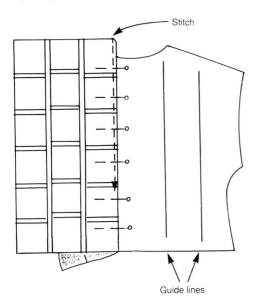

Guide lines

Figure 6-9.
To make flat felled seam, stitch standard ⅝" seam.

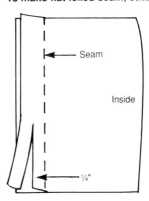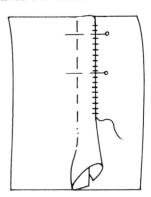

A. Trim one side only.

B. Fold under remaining allowance and stitch in place.

Flat Felled Seams

If a seam isn't too bulky, you may be able to use a flat felled seam finish. Follow these steps:

1. After the seam has been joined through all the thicknesses, trim one side to ¼" (Figure 6-9).
2. Fold the remaining long side over the short one. (Remove the batting if possible.) Pin-baste.
3. Hand stitch in place with small stitches. I use blind hemming stitches placed ⅛" to ¼" apart.

Bound Seams

If a seam is bulky, a bound seam will be easier to make than a flat felled seam. It takes longer and requires adding an additional piece of fabric to the seam. To apply binding to your seam:

1. Cut a strip of straight or bias fabric 1½" to 1¾" wide and a little longer than the sum total of the seams to be bound (Figure 6-10).
2. Press the strip in half lengthwise, being careful to not stretch it. (Stretching occurs when the iron is moved back and forth in a scrubbing motion rather than an up and down motion.)
3. Along the raw edges, create a second fold, or crease line, ¼" wide.
4. Line the folded crease line up with the original seam line. Pin or hand-baste the binding in place (Figure 6-11).
5. Machine stitch through all the layers, making sure to stitch right on top of the crease line.

Figure 6-10.
To make seam binding:

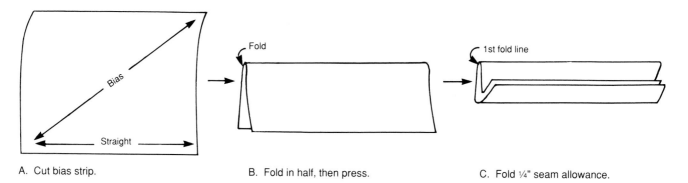

A. Cut bias strip.

B. Fold in half, then press.

C. Fold ¼" seam allowance.

Figure 6-11.
To apply seam binding:

A. Baste binding to
seam allowance.

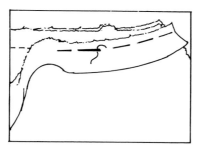

B. Stitch in place.

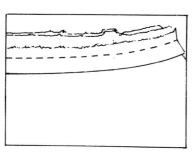

Figure 6-12.
To trim bound seam:

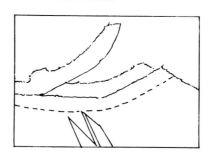

A. Trim outside
seam to ¼".

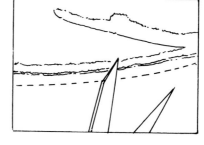

B. Trim middle
layer to ⅜".

6. Trim the seam allowance away, being careful to leave at least ¼" (Figure 6-12). You may want to stagger the seams to reduce bulk, but again, never cut to less than ¼".

7. If any area is curved, clip into the remaining seam allowance so it will be released to lie flat. Be careful to stop cutting before the seam is reached. An ⅛" away is safest. Several small clips are better than one big one (Figure 6-13).

8. To complete the binding application, turn the seam and binding to the side and pin the folded edge of the binding to the lining (Figure 6-14).

9. To make sure the bound seam lies flat and is unnoticeable from the right side, run the middle finger of your left hand along the seam on the right side as you are pinning the strip in place. (Left-handers will reverse this process.)

10. Secure with blind hemming. In all the above procedures, you may use straight-grain binding if your seams are straight. However, if you will be binding the outside edge in bias, you may want to cut everything bias.

If it is necessary to piece your strip, it will lie better if you piece it by sewing a diagonal seam. This distributes the seam bulk over a greater area rather than having the bulk of the additional seam all at the same spot.

Figure 6-13.
To clip seam allowance on curves:

A. Take small snips, stopping ⅛" from seam.

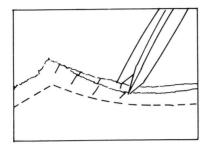

B. Curves will be released and open.

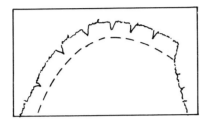

Figure 6-14.
To finish binding:

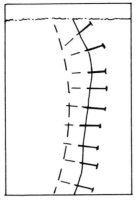

A. Pin in place.   B. Blind stitch.

Binding Outside Edges

Often the outside edges of vests and jackets are bound. To bind an outside edge, do the following:

1. Cut adequate bias. Since curves are usually involved, you will want the flexibility of a bias binding. If you want the bias to show as a trim at the edge, cut it 2" wide; if you prefer to pull it to the inside and have it not show, cut it the same width as the inside bindings.
2. Press the binding in half lengthwise: press a second fold or crease, ¼" from the raw edges.
3. Machine-baste a line of stitching ⅝" away from the edges to be bound. (If your pattern doesn't have standard seams, check to make sure how close to the edge the pattern suggests the binding be sewn.) This line of stitching will be used as a guide.
4. Line up the crease line of your folded binding with the stitched guide line. Pin or hand-baste in place. When applying binding to an edge, I have the best results when I take the time to hand-baste it in place first. This is particularly important around the lower armhole, around the neck, and if there are curves at the bottom or top at the center opening.
5. Machine stitch through all the layers.
6. Trim sewn edge to ¼".
7. If you want your bias trim to show, fold it carefully over to meet the stitching line on the back side.
8. If you don't want the trim to show, pull it all the way to the back side. Pin the binding in place, being careful to even out any fullness.
9. Handsew the binding in place with blind stitches ⅛" to ¼" apart.

If your bias strips need to be continuous, as around an armhole or an entire outer edge, decide ahead of time where to start and stop. When selecting a spot, try to be as inconspicuous as possible. Don't locate it at a seam as there will be too much bulk. I usually choose a spot about 1" to 2" from the side seam on the back side of the garment.

Also make sure to fold under a ¼" edge at the end to begin with when you start positioning the binding in place. When you come around to the beginning again, leave an adequate lap-over before you snip off the binding. I usually leave between ½" to 1" extra. The end can be neatly stitched in place when you handsew the back side of the binding.

Since the eye will naturally notice what is happening at center front, particularly the part nearest your face, make sure your binding application is especially neat here. Sometimes problems are caused by curling at the edge if there are curves rather than a right angle where the direction of the edges shifts from the neck to center front and center front to the lower edge. One solution is to change these curves to right angles before the garment is cut out.

If the center front corners are right angles, they can be finished with mitered corners, but I much prefer an alternative method. I use two strips of binding attached separately, much as the Amish do in binding their quilt corners:

1. Following the previously described method, sew a strip of binding to the right side of the garment neck. Trim the edges to ¼" and trim the ends even (Figure 6-15).
2. Turn the binding to the lining side and handstitch it in place.

3. Repeat Steps 1 and 2 for the lower edge.
4. Pin the binding to the front edges, overhanging ½" at the ends. Sew.
5. Turn the binding to the lining side, and tuck in any overhangs. Handstitch it in place.

Figure 6-15.
To apply binding to garments with right-angle front edges:

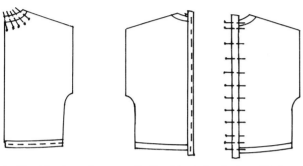

A. Pin strips to neck and to lower edges. Stitch.

B. Pin strips to front edge. Stitch.

FINISHING TOUCHES

As a teacher who has graded more garments than she can count, I suggest a final check when you think everything is finished. Check for stray basting threads and any loose thread ends that you might have missed along the way.

Take a good photograph or slide while the garment is fresh and new for documentation purposes. The photos can be used to enter shows, as part of a personal portfolio, for insurance, or to add to a "brag book" to share with other quilters.

You may also enjoy using the photo in making a collage for your workroom. In addition to a picture of the finished project, you could include sketches, notes, and fabric swatches and mount them all in a Plexiglas box. Though your garment provides tangible evidence of your completed project, it's fun to look back on the steps along the way. The collage can inspire you as you begin the process all over again, because now you know you can do it. Once you've made one, you've just *begun* creating wearable art for real people.

BIBLIOGRAPHY

Many of the books noted here have been self-published or are available from less well-known publishers; for those, I have included addresses. Contact the author/publisher directly if you are unable to locate a copy in your local quilt store or public library.

Betzina, Sandra. *Power Sewing*. 1985. Sandra Betzina, World Trade Center, Suite 275H, San Francisco, CA 94111.

Bishop, Robert, and Carter Houck. *All Flags Flying: American Patriotic Quilts as Expressions of Liberty*. 1986. E. P. Dutton, New York.

Ericson, Lois. *Belts...Waisted Sculpture*. 1984. Eric's Press, Box 1680, Tahoe City, CA 95730.

Ericson, Lois. *Fabrics...Reconstructed: A Collection of Surface Changes*. 1985. Eric's Press, Box 1680, Tahoe City, CA 95730.

Frode, Diane Ericson, and Lois Ericson. *Sewing it Yourself: A Myriad of Techniques for Creative Sewing*. 1981. Eric's Press, Box 1680, Tahoe City, CA 95730.

Hargrave, Harriet. *Heirloom Machine Quilting*. 1987. Dale Burdett, 5455 Garden Grove Boulevard, Westminister, CA 92683.

Herbort, Diane E., and Susan Greenhut. *The Quiltwear Book: Country Quilted Garments that Work 9 to 5 —and Beyond*. 1988. EPM Publications, Inc., 1003 Turkey Run Road, McLean, VA 22101.

Millard, Debra. *A Quilter's Guide to Fabric Dyeing*. 1984. Debra Millard Lunn, 1225 Garfield Street, Denver, CO 80206.

Ogawa, Hiroko. "Embroidery from Japan's Snow Country." *Threads Magazine,* #18, Aug./Sept. 1988.

Ota, Kimi. *Sashiko Quilting*. 1981. 10030 61st Avenue, South Seattle, WA 98178.

Thelen, Marilyn. *Sew Big!* 1980. Palmer/Pletch Associates, P.O. Box 8422, Portland, OR 97207.

Thompson, Sue. *Decorative Dressmaking*. 1985. Rodale Press, Emmaus, PA.

Appendix — Sources

The Cotton Patch
Carolie Hensley
1025 Brown Avenue
Lafayette, CA 94549
415/284-1177
Pushed-neutral kits, "Shibui Stripes" by Mary Mashuta, "Lines" and "Mood Indigo" Collections by Roberta Horton, quilting supplies including Illse pins, etc.

Fabricart
Barb Engelking
6600 Cypress Avenue
Superior, WI 54880
715/392-2075
Hand-marbled fabric

Kasuri Dyeworks
1959 Shattuck Avenue
Berkeley, CA 94704
415/841-4509
Sashiko stencils and thread

Debra Millard Lunn
1225 Garfield Street
Denver, CO 80206
303/377-1913
Hand-dyed cottons (solids and patterns)

Needlearts International
P.O. Box 6447-T
Glendale, CA 91205
213/227-1535
Sashiko stencils and thread

Omnigrid
Randal Schafer
P.O. Box 3076
Lynnwood, WA 98046

206/743-9142 or 800/543-4206
"Quiltersgrid" rulers, marked for both light and dark colors, both right- and left-handed users

Portapress
Studio North, Inc.
P.O. Box 463
Manistee, MI 49660
Portable ironing boards

Q Snap Frame
Lamb Art Press
Route 1, Box 156A
Parsons, TN 38363
Portable, break-apart quilting frames

Shades, Inc.
Stacy Michell
2880 Holcomb Bridge Road, Suite B-9
Alpharetta, GA 30201
404/587-1706
Hand-dyed cottons and silks (solids, special effects, and textures)

Smith Quilting Stencils
13502 Cedar Circle East
Sumner, WA 98390
206/897-9418
Quilting stencils (adaptable for sashiko)

Uni-Unique Products
P.O. Box 2606
Rohnert Park, CA 94928
707/585-9337
"A-Just-A-Table System," modular sewing tables, mats, accessories, etc.

ABOUT THE AUTHOR

Mary Mashuta's love of fabric and color began in childhood and led to two degrees in Home Economics. Taking up quilting in the 1970s, she quickly became an active member of the San Francisco Bay Area quilt community. In the mid-1980s, Mary embarked on a career change, and began to work full-time on her quilt-related interests, including designing, writing, and teaching.

Mary enjoys creating "story" quilts detailing her experiences, and loves to help others discover how to make their own quilts more personal. Her award-winning creations have been shown both across the country and internationally.

Professional experience in the interior design field fostered an avid interest in quilt studios. Her informative articles on these and other quilting topics have appeared in several national quilting magazines.

Mary particularly enjoys making art-to-wear and is a repeat Fairfield Processing/Concord Fabric Fashion Show participant. Her background in custom dressmaking accounts for her skill and reputation for fine finishing details. As a teacher, Mary has worked tirelessly to share her ideas (including the innovative color concept of pushed neutrals), skills, and enthusiasms.